MW00513862

_____Valerie_____ ____

Gift of Tennis

A Cup of Tea & Other Court Thoughts

VALERIE CLARKE

Foreword by Gyata Stormon

Art & Design by Jennifer Hooley

GIFT OF TENNIS • VALERIE CLARKE
www.giftoftennis.com

This edition first published in 2020 in the United States by Voncee Ventures
P.O. Box 255, Cazenovia, NY 13035

ISBN: 978-0-578-76959-2 (paperback)

Copyediting by Tina Grenis

Tennis content editing by Gyata Stormon
www.gyatastormon.com

Logo designs and graphics consulting by Shelley Holmes

Website design and photography by Andrea Elliott
www.andreamariemedia.com

For my students — Past, Present and Future

Gift of Tennis

Table of Contents

Gift of Tennis

Key

TECHNICAL

At the Core of It
Back to Basics
Banana Split Step
Energizer Bunny
Follow Through
From Chaos to Consistency
Get a Grip
Laid-Back Dude
Patience Is a Virtue
Practice with Purpose
Tennis Technician
Tip for the Server
To Everything, Turn, Turn, Turn
You Be the Judge

MENTAL

A Cup of Tea and a Tennis Ball
Believe
Do You Mind?
Every Breath You Take
Focal or Vocal?
Gratitude Attitude
Inside Out
Laughter Is the Best Medicine
Slowing Down Time
Under Pressure

TACTICAL

Eenie Meenie Minie Moe
Get Back!
Make a Plan
No Place Like Home
Profile Your Opponent
Second Chances
Take a Stand
Taking Sides
Tiebreaks
Trust and Teamwork

PRACTICAL

An Honest Mistake
Communication Revelation
Earth, Wind, and Fire
From San Juan to Yukon
Listen to Your Body
On the Line
One Court Thought at a Time
Pacemaker
Tennis Diet
Warm Up Before the Warm Up
What's Love Got to Do With It?

Gift of Tennis

Foreword

When Valerie Clarke joined my beginners class in 2016, I knew she was something special. She played outside of class with a friend from the get-go and in addition, practiced by herself on the ball machine. When faced with tennis elbow, she played left handed during her recovery. I'd never seen anything like the passion and dedication exhibited by my new student.

I calculate that Valerie has easily had a decade's worth of tennis experience since she took up the game four years ago. She has studied, taken private and group lessons, played and practiced almost daily, competed at every opportunity, and programmed our PlayMate ball machine with more than 50 tactically sound drills.

Valerie's tactical understanding and attention to detail made her an obvious choice to be the tennis content editor for my book, *On the Ball*. Her insightful comments on the many versions of the book gave me confidence that it would be accessible to all levels of players, even those just beginning their tennis journey.

After a couple of years of playing, Valerie's desire to share her love for the game brought her to coaching. One of the attributes that makes Valerie a wonderful coach is that although she has traveled far beyond the beginner stage in her own play, she remembers how it felt to step on the court for the first time. Notably, Valerie expanded our adult beginners program to include a Novice League that provides playing experience and guidance to our newest players. The weekly emails she sent to this group provided the starting point for *Gift of Tennis*.

Gift of Tennis was crafted with the same enthusiasm and thoroughness that Valerie brings to anything she takes on. The book is a joy to read and provides plenty of opportunity for growth in a willing reader. I couldn't have been happier when Valerie teamed up with Jennifer Hooley to illustrate and design the book. In addition to being an artist, Jennifer is a lovely player and successful coach in her own right. Their co-creation will delight and inspire you for years to come.

Gyata Stormon
Tennis and life coach
Author of *On the Ball: Doubles Tennis Tactics for Recreational Players*

Certified US PTR and Canadian TPA Coach
Canadian Doubles Champion
M.A. Sociology
Certified Forrest Yoga Teacher

Foreword

Gift of Tennis

Preface

This book was inspired by my interaction with the Novice League tennis group that I coach at the Manlius YMCA in Central New York.

In 2018, we created the Novice League for players who were just beginning to play games or who were returning to tennis after a break. Players met once or twice per week for doubles tennis match play. It was my privilege, as a newly certified tennis instructor, to coach the group as they played, teaching them various doubles tactics and techniques, work which continues to this day.

I guide them through match play, help them become familiar with the mechanics involved in scoring, playing sets, changing ends of the court, and provide feedback about their strengths and weaknesses. When needed, I play in to make up a foursome.

For the first eighteen months, I sent the Novice League players a weekly email that included one tennis topic. The topic may have been inspired by their match play the previous week, or it may have originated from my own tennis journey—perhaps something I discovered during match play or a "eureka" moment I had in a lesson with my coach. I called these topics "court thoughts" and encouraged the players to embrace one court thought at a time as they expanded their skills.

The court thoughts were enthusiastically received by the group, and a few of the players asked if they could share them with their other tennis friends who weren't part of the Novice League. I was pleased they found them to be of value and was encouraged to collect them together in this book for easy access to a wider audience.

Over the past two years, the Novice League and I have grown together, and somewhere along the journey, a couple of them nicknamed me "#gift of tennis" out of gratitude for helping them grow as tennis players. I can assure you, the feeling was mutual, as this group has been a gift to me as well. They have helped me grow as a coach and have given me great pleasure as I watch them improve and discover the same joy for tennis that I feel.

It is for these reasons that this book has been christened *Gift of Tennis*, and it is my hope that you will feel it is a gift to you as well.

Treat playing
tennis like
having a
cup of
tea

Gift of Tennis

Introduction

I've always considered myself a lifelong learner, ready to take on a new subject, driven by a passionate curiosity to know more. By contrast, I have not embraced learning new physical skills with the same determination, enthusiasm, or courage. Having little to no training in sports, I lacked confidence and felt more comfortable avoiding sports altogether. This is why it required a great leap of faith for me to leave my comfort zone and take on the challenge of learning to play tennis as an adult.

In the beginning, tennis lessons were overwhelming with all of the various aspects I had to take on board—judging the ball bounce, changing my grip, setting up correctly to the shot, hitting out in front, powering the shot with my legs, finishing the swing with a full follow-through, and recovering to start the cycle over again. There were many occasions where I felt my brain would explode if I tried to cram in one more thought.

Over time, I discovered *how to learn* physical skills, where we must connect our brains with our bodies, a process I found to be vastly different to acquiring academic information. On the tennis court, I became aware that my mind can only focus on one thought at a time, something I've come to refer to as a "court thought." This meant that when I was learning something complex, I gained more by practicing one aspect of it until I achieved a moderate level of proficiency, before moving on to another. Ultimately, this systematic approach, "one *court thought* at a time", sharpened my focus and helped me to progress along my tennis journey.

Learning to play tennis was a gift, something I wish to share with other adults. Because I can vividly remember how it was to be a beginner, feeling overwhelmed with the volume of new information imparted upon us, I help my students simplify what they're learning. I break down the tennis skills into individual components in order to facilitate focusing on one court thought at a time.

Gift of Tennis is a compilation of court thoughts with topics that span four categories: technical, tactical, mental, and practical aspects of tennis. Becoming a well-rounded doubles tennis player involves study of all of these topics. Although this book is written for recreational tennis players at the novice and intermediate levels, it contains nuggets of information even advanced players may find valuable.

Several court thoughts in this book were inspired by my own tennis experience, such as thoughts about breath, nerves, and focus under pressure. Many have evolved organically through teaching. Some of the court thoughts focus on where to stand and what areas of the court to cover, while others delve into the "how to" such as how to hold and swing the racquet for the most effective shots. A few topics explore and clarify rules and conventions.

The court thoughts in *Gift of Tennis*, each one its own chapter, can be used as a guide as you broaden and improve your tennis proficiencies. Each court thought has been assigned to one of the four categories with a corresponding *symbol*: technical—*tennis racquet and ball*, tactical—*home*, mental—*cup of tea*, practical—*the egg character*. They are also listed by category in the Key at the front of the book. Many of the topics are appropriate to share with your doubles partner so you can progress together.

Use these court thoughts to inspire your practice, inform your court knowledge, and enhance your joy as you travel along the path of your own tennis journey. You may even find that the principles underlying many of the court thoughts cross over into various aspects of your everyday life.

Believe

Gift of Tennis

A Cup of Tea and a Tennis Ball

Use your time on the tennis court to relieve your mind
of the stresses life can bring.

What do a cup of tea and a tennis ball have in common? They're both tools you can use to relieve stress. They're both points of focus you can use to take your mind off thoughts that exhaust you when you dwell on them. A tea break or a tennis break—you can use them both in similar ways.

About 25 years ago when I was living in England, we had our first baby, and my husband was working a couple of hours away during the week. One night when I was up late, I heard noises and discovered a burglary was in action downstairs. With my heartbeat thumping loudly in my ears, I phoned the police, and when they arrived the burglars fled. I was very shaken up.

The two police constables proceeded to mend the door as they took details from me for their report. About five minutes into the interview, one of them suggested, "Why don't you brew some tea, love?"

Tea was the last thing I thought I needed in the middle of the night, so I politely declined the offer. "Well, if it's not too much trouble, we'd like one," he persisted. So I dropped into tea-making mode, put the kettle on, got out the cups, and prepared the pot.

As I went about this ritual, my nerves began to recover, and by the time I served the tea 10 minutes later, I was restored to a sense of calmness. Later, I deduced that those police constables probably didn't really desire a cup of tea, but they knew that making the tea would be a good distraction for me. I've since realized that putting the kettle on is a common way the English respond when something stressful intersects their daily lives.

Fast forward more than two decades later...I had planned to meet my longtime friend on the tennis court early one morning to practice. Just before I'd left my house, I had received some disturbing news from my son who was living a few thousand miles away. It upset me, and as I was driving to the tennis court, I was wondering how in the world I was going to be able to concentrate on a tennis game when I was so distracted with my son's problem.

I decided it was best to get on with the game and not tell my friend what had happened, mainly because I feared that talking about it might make me break down and cry. I would just have to try my best to put the problem on hold, play, and not fall apart.

What I didn't expect was that playing tennis had a huge therapeutic effect on my state of mind. Once I was on the court and focused on the little yellow ball, there was no other room in my mind to contemplate my son's upsetting news. It was just me, my friend, and the tennis ball. An hour and a half later, I felt refreshed and renewed because, without intending to, playing tennis had given my mind a welcome break.

It was then that I realized the power an activity such as tennis could have in providing an escape. I'd always heard that exercise was a good stress reliever, but I never understood until then how this actually worked.

I hope that you will consider using tennis, not only as an avenue for physical fitness and social interaction, but as a stress reliever, too. It's important to carve out time for yourself, especially when you are bombarded with all of the demands in life. Playing tennis can help you to fill your cup, restore your soul, and prepare you to face the rest of your day feeling glad you took the time for yourself.

An Honest Mistake

Assume your opponent is honest and be generous with your responses.

Have you ever been on the court with a player who continuously makes close line calls? How did you handle it...perhaps you're that player? Do you tend to make calls more often in your favor when it's an important point or when you're down in games won? Be honest with yourself.

Tennis can awaken a competitive side and bring out the best in us. This can heighten our focus, make us quicker to respond to various shots, and build our confidence. Unfortunately, it can also bring out our worst, leading to more aggressive behavior or selective perception as to how players see things. Competition may make us behave with more intensity about a questionable line call, double bounce, or other fault such as touching the net.

We should come onto the court in good faith, believing that those we play with are honest. If we think that a player is repeatedly making bad line calls, instead of assuming it's deliberately dishonest, assume that player is just bad at judging where the ball bounced. Don't jump to the conclusion that she is purposely cheating.

The majority of bad calls, or failing to make a call on yourself, are most likely simple mistakes of judgement or perception. For example, a ball that appears *out* to one player may seem *in* to another.

The best practice is to let most things go rather than challenging your opponent. Focus on the present moment, not the past. Minimize a dispute in your mind and move on so that you continue to play well. No matter how much you may want to win, don't let things escalate to awkward or ugly.

Once you question a call or an action, the atmosphere on the court may change, and negative vibes might result. A confrontation may bring on feelings of anger or anxiety and distract you so that you are no longer focused on the next point. Ironically, it may be you who gets thrown off and feels like the match was spoiled.

However, there are times when you'll want to speak up. If one player makes several bad calls during a set, bring it to her attention but do so diplomatically, asking the question, "Are you sure?" By asking this question, the opponent may be more careful the next time she makes a line call.

I reserve this verbal response when my partner and I are feeling fairly certain that the other player has made two or three bad line calls in a set. I don't say something the first or even second time I think she was wrong. Initially, I give her the benefit of the doubt.

My doubles partner and I played a woman several times in USTA competition who often responded to our line calls with the comment, "Boy, that looked in to me." She usually did this when she was down in the match and frustrated with her team's performance. We were annoyed because she was judging her ball from the far end of the court, and it felt like she was accusing us of dishonesty. The frequency of her challenges became a real downer and spoiled the match for us. It didn't look like she was having much fun, either.

Be conservative with your court behavior and follow the guidelines below.

For line calls:

- Don't question a line call unless it happens multiple times in the same match and you feel that the team is regularly making bad calls.

- Remember that your opponent is usually closer to the ball than you or your partner, so she probably has a better view of where the ball bounced.

- When you question a line call, your opponent will probably not choose to retract her call, but it puts her on notice that you want her to be more careful when she judges the ball the next time.

For double-bounces:

- If a player hits a ball that has double-bounced, it's up to that player to admit it; it's not for the opponents to make that call.

- If you think you saw a double-bounce, it may or may not have actually occurred. Sometimes it's an illusion that a ball has double-bounced because the opponent's racquet hits the ground as she makes contact after the first bounce.

- If the opponent doesn't call a double-bounce on the ball she hits, then assume it's a good ball and stay focused so you can respond to her shot. Don't make the mistake of assuming that the point is over. It may be worth commenting between points, "I thought the point had already ended because it looked to me like the ball had double bounced," or something diplomatic like that.

For touching the ball as a mis-hit:

- If the ball grazes your racquet as it whizzes past you, even ever so slightly, and no one else perceives this but you, be honest and immediately own up as that's considered a hit, and the point goes to the other team. This will garner good faith between you and your opponents.

- It's up to you to call, "It touched my racquet." The opponent is not allowed to make that call, but they may have noticed what happened, so be honest immediately.

For touching the net:

- If you touch the net at any time during a point or *break the plane* (when your racquet crosses over the net and contacts the ball on the opponent's side of the court), be honest about it.

- Again, this is a call we must make on ourselves. It's not for our opponents to call this fault.

For hitting another player:

- If a player sends a ball that hits another player, realize that this was most likely an accident and don't take offense. Tennis is a game with balls flying through the air, so we must accept there is a risk of being hit.

- If you're the player who sent the ball, quickly say sorry to affirm it was an accident. Accidents happen, and it's important that everyone is forgiving, but don't dwell on it.

- However, if you notice you hit players frequently, you're probably being somewhat reckless, aiming too close to players without having enough control. Until your control improves, aim for bigger targets away from your opponents.

In general, keep your assumptions positive and give your opponents the benefit of the doubt, recognizing that we all make mistakes. Tennis is a game we play to have fun.

Don't turn it into a battle if you disagree over a line call. Let most things go so that you can remain focused on your game and derive the pleasure it generates. If you can follow these guidelines, your time on the court will most likely render more positive tennis experiences. (For more about line calls, see my discussion in Court Thought, "On the Line.")

Thoughts for Today
① for every match, two practices
② know the score
③ keep your eye on the ball
④ get a grip
⑤ Trust your Shots

At the Core of It

Use your feet, legs, and core of your body
to generate the power for your groundstrokes.

When I started tennis, it took me more than two years to begin to consistently engage my core—including my feet, thighs, glutes, hips, waist, and abs—in my groundstrokes. I tend to be one who overthinks things when I'm learning.

Like many beginning players, I had the habit of muscling the ball with my arm. I might have continued executing my groundstrokes this way for much longer if not for a case of tennis elbow. This injury forced me to re-examine how I was hitting the ball and find a way to link my arm to the rest of my body.

Over time, and with a great deal of dedicated practice, I learned how to connect with my legs and core and use my entire body to send my shots. Improving my technique not only made tennis feel easier, it made me feel confident on the court, as though I'd been playing for years.

If you're new to tennis, it's common to be fixated on your arm and racquet when learning to execute strokes, almost as if the rest of your body doesn't exist. Your thoughts are probably clogged with notions of racquet take-back, swing path, impact point, hitting zone, and follow through. Adult learners are especially cerebral when learning, analyzing each component, and trying to execute shots with their brains. In doing so, they often isolate their racquet arm from the rest of their body.

Children, on the other hand, are often more natural when learning the basics of tennis. I have concluded that the primary reason for this is because they are more focused on the ball than on their arm. They allow their bodies to execute their groundstrokes because they aren't trying to control each component of the shot with their thoughts. Instead, they *feel* the shot.

As a result, their body parts work together as a unit to hit the ball. They push off with their feet and legs to drive the swing, using the core of their bodies to move the racquet. The power is generated by some of the largest muscles of the body, and the outcome is an effortless shot.

There are several steps I have learned to connect the various parts of my body in order to generate a smooth, easy swing. First, as the ball approaches, I move to the right place on the court and stop before I hit the ball so that I can push off with my feet to start the swing; it's much easier to push off when you've stopped running.

It's also crucial to get turned sideways as I set up to the shot because it positions me to rotate naturally, using my core as I swing. Another helpful tip is to have my belly button facing the target at the end of the stroke, like you do with a golf swing. Once I added these cues into my shots and practiced each, one at a time, with lots and lots of repetitions, my groundstrokes began to feel less demanding.

You can begin from your living room with ghost swings. First, set up your feet a little wider than your hip distance. Your legs should not be crossed over each other, but rather more open, so that you can properly rotate your core.

For a forehand swing, if you're right-handed, push off with your right foot (if you're left-handed, push off with your left foot) and feel the movement come from your legs and through your core as your body twists around and your racquet moves through its swing path. The same can be done to practice the backhand, only push off with the opposite foot.

Self-feeding balls is an instructional tool I've discovered to help my students feel the shot and engage their core. Self-feeding isolates the sending phase of the shot cycle. (For more information about the different phases of the shot cycle, see my discussion in Court Thought, "Slowing Down Time.") It allows you to focus on hitting without having to judge the bounce of the ball that's moving towards you, as you must do during a rally or a session with a ball machine.

To self feed, set up sideways to the court, drop the ball into your hitting zone, about 45 degrees out from your body, and drive the stroke from your lower body and core. The racquet should move across the front of your body as you finish the stroke. Pick a target, such as the area deep crosscourt, and move your racquet in that direction without any tension in your arm.

You can use self-feeding for backhand practice as well. Be patient; it's a little trickier. If you hit two-handed, you will need to toss the ball up higher to give yourself more time to place both hands on the grip. This will also buy you a bit of time to set up and take the racquet back. Self-feeding a one-handed backhand also requires a higher toss because you need a bit more time as the tossing arm moves out of the way while your other arm takes the racquet back.

Once you've acquired the feel of the shot, you can engage in rallies with a practice partner. If you don't have a partner to hit with, consider using a ball machine to feed you balls. Connecting your feet, legs, hips, and core to your racquet arm to generate a powerful swing that feels effortless may take thousands of balls over time.

Be patient and stick with it; gradually your consistency will improve. Manage your enthusiasm and be careful not to zealously overdo the task at the beginning, as overuse injuries can cause long-term setbacks in your tennis journey.

Enjoy your practice in small, focused increments. You'll find, as I did, that engaging your core in your groundstrokes will improve your technique, allow you to hit with greater power, and reduce the stress on your racquet arm. Operating your body as a unit will bring about optimal performance and help to boost your game to the next level. You may even start to feel and look like someone who has been playing tennis for years!

Back to Basics

When things aren't going well in your game,
go back to the basics to make adjustments.

Some days, we are awesome on the court. Our shots are effective, we win more points, and we think, "Wow, my lessons, drills, and practice have finally paid off." Then, the very next day, we get out on the court full of confidence...and our game seems to fall apart.

Because we've been hitting so well before this, it's a shock. We find ourselves flustered, puzzled, and frustrated. In contrast to the *unstoppable* feelings we had the previous day, we finish this match feeling completely deflated.

What can you do when you are in this situation on the court? I suggest you go back to the basics. Here are some focus points you can use to help you assess and identify the root cause for your ailing performance.

The list is extensive, and it's not advised that you focus on all of these things at once. Consider one idea at a time as you seek your solution.

Breath: Use your breath to help to calm your senses and erase your frustration.

- Take your time between points. Don't let anxiety ramp up your pace.
- Take a deep breath and exhale. Feel the tension leave your body.
- Feel joy as you remind yourself you're glad to be on the court.

Eye on the ball: Are you remembering to keep your eye on the ball all the way through impact? This is probably my favorite tip of all. So basic yet so important! It is very easy to watch the ball come into your hitting zone, then transfer your gaze to the target as you hit it instead of watching the ball through impact. I cannot tell you the number of times this one principle has made a huge difference to my execution. If I watch the target, I execute inconsistently (often a mis-hit). If I watch the ball, I execute my stroke beautifully 90 percent of the time.

- Glance at your target, then watch the ball, knowing in your mind's eye where the target is, but no longer looking at it.

- I find that the 10-minute warm-up is the best time to get myself zoned in on the ball, making a deliberate effort to watch the ball on each impact. This small practice makes me much more focused during the match.

Active feet: Are you keeping your feet moving during the point, even if you're not the player hitting the ball?

- Move your feet while you're waiting to return the serve, during the point, and even in between points. This will keep you alert and in a state of readiness.

- When you don't feel like you're playing your best, it's easy to become despondent. "Fake it until you make it," my coach has reminded me. Before long, you may feel your usual zest for the game return.

Court position: Are you recovering to your correct home after you hit the ball? Pay attention to where you are on the court after every point, especially one you've lost. If you find you were in the wrong place, make an effort to correct that in the points ahead.

- As the baseline player, are you standing *behind* the baseline? If you are drawn in on a short ball, are you recovering to your *service line home*, or are you mistakenly setting up home in the transition zone (no man's land)?

- As the net player, are you at your home in the *middle of the service box*, or are you hanging too far back? When you see the ball going to the other net player, are you *backing up toward the T* ready to defend? If the ball lands out wide on the other end of the court, are you *moving over* to anticipate the opponent sending the ball down the line?

- Are you remembering to recover immediate. there watching your shot to see where it land

Groundstrokes: Do you need to adjust your grip, impact

- Are you making contact with the ball out in fro. your stance? When the ball bounces, don't move you and the ball so you can swing without feeling

- Are you finishing the stroke with a follow-throu. between points to reinforce the proper stroke path f.

- If your balls are traveling high and beyond the end of using the correct grip.

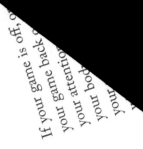

Volleys: Do you need to adjust your grip, ready position, or impac.

- Are you using the proper continental grip?

- Is your racquet held high enough in your ready position?

- Are you making contact with the ball out in front of you (not beside you)?

- Is your volley a short punch or block with your racquet? Or are you swinging it? Remember, a volley is like catching the ball on your strings and throwing it back. There is no backswing.

- Executing ghost strokes between points is a good way to reinforce proper form.

Serve: Take your time to prepare yourself to serve, including getting setup, calming yourself, and sharpening your focus.

- Are you set up correctly behind the baseline with back foot parallel to the baseline?

- Are you executing a good ball toss? Are you hitting a bad ball toss?

- Are you focused on the ball at impact?

- Are you relaxed?

something has derailed it, try using one or two focus points to get
on track during a match. Focusing on one thing at a time will help move
away from your negative thoughts about how poorly you're playing and into
which is where we play our best tennis. Stay focused on the present and leave
mistakes in the past. Once you've succeeded with this process, your confidence—and
with it, your game—will return.

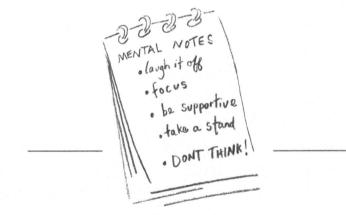

Banana Split Step

Remember to split step each time your opponent hits the ball.

I was up at dawn one day, observing the transition between night and sunrise over a calm lake. It was peaceful, full of the promise of new beginnings, and probably my favorite time of day.

The dawn offers me that feeling of calm, tinged with the hope of a positive outcome within moments. It's a fresh beginning as I'm focused on what is about to happen—the sky brightening, perhaps an increase from blue to pink to yellow. It's the centering moment to my day, just before the sun pops up over the trees.

I'm reminded of a similar feeling I have at the dawn of a new tennis match, set, game, or even just a new point. The start of each point offers a fresh beginning. When I'm properly in the moment, I am not thinking about my last point, my last mistake, or winning the game. I'm calm, focused on what is about to happen on the court. I'm watching the ball and ready for anything; the ball may come to my forehand, my backhand, high, low, short, deep, fast, slow, with spin.

Then I take a breath and clear my mind of clutter, keeping open to all possibilities. I'm in the centering moment of the point. I have a single focus (the ball), I'm standing in ready position, and as my opponent hits the ball, I split step.

The split step is a key component of this centering moment. It's a gentle hop on the balls of my feet that prepares my body to respond to the ball, whichever way it comes to me or my partner. It activates the body in preparation to move toward the ball. When I regularly use a split step, I play better. My mind and body are energized that bit sooner than if I were just standing grounded to the court.

Listening to "Top 5 Lessons from Indian Wells," an episode from the Essential Tennis Podcast (Westermann, 2019), I was interested in how much emphasis was placed on the split step. Westermann believes it is the most fundamental element to perform on the court from which all else depends. He also said it is not coached very often or practiced well in the lower levels of recreational tennis. He had a player attend one of his clinics who had spent $4,000 in tennis lessons up to that point and said she had never even heard of the split step.

I am grateful that my coach taught me the split step at the beginning of my training. At first, it felt a bit odd and wasn't always easy to remember, but as with other tennis skills, practicing it over time paid off. Initially, I focused on split stepping when I was receiving serve. Right away, I could perceive the benefit to the timing of my return shots.

After lots of practice, over months of playing, it finally became automatic. However, it's taken me several years to incorporate it more consistently into my entire game, and not just when I'm receiving serve.

Ideally, we split step each time our opponent hits the ball throughout the entire point, game, set, and match. In fact, in doubles, once the point has begun, both players should split step every time the opponent hits the ball, even though only one of the partners will receive it.

Although our feet should always be moving on the court in anticipation of the next shot, the split step is an additional deliberate hop we execute simultaneously with the opponent's racquet striking the ball. It helps to keep us focused on the present as we watch our opponent hit the ball, and it prepares us to move in any direction to get to the ball for our next shot.

Incorporating the split step requires discipline, conscious effort, and many repetitions. A good starting point for practicing the split step is during mini tennis in the warm-up. Make *split step* your court thought so that each time your opponent hits the ball, you practice deliberately executing it. Note whether or not you start to feel your response times for each shot are improved.

Next, practice it when rallying with a partner from the baseline. You can even practice it if you're hitting on a ball machine by making your split step each time the ball machine makes a noise as it launches the next ball. Have faith and stick with it. Over time, the split step will become automatic for you, transform your tennis timing, and enhance your performance.

Like the dawn of each day, the split step is a reset for each shot. It assists you in focusing on the present moment as you watch your opponent hit the ball. It helps you to move out of the past where you can leave your mistakes behind. The split step energizes you, mentally and physically, like a spark plug, igniting your engine. Practicing it may feel contrived at first, but dedication to assimilating it into your game will create a new beginning in your tennis journey and lead to greater enjoyment on the court.

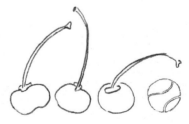

Believe!

Believe in your ability. Whether it is a shot you want to make or a new skill you want to master, consciously tell yourself you can do it.

If you grew up believing in the tooth fairy, you may harken back to memories of your childhood when the magic of make-believe was as real as the tooth that you lost. When a loose tooth would fall out, my daughter ritually placed it under her pillow, sometimes accompanied by a note for the tooth fairy. Time and time again, she was thrilled by her discovery of a small gift the next morning that the fairy had left in payment.

Her belief in the tooth fairy went on for years until one day when she was digging through my closet and found the box of notes she'd left for the tooth fairy; her illusion was shattered. She was devastated. Until that moment, she'd never doubted that the tooth fairy was real because she wanted to believe.

Belief can be powerful. It can make the difference between success and failure, simply by the mindset you choose. This can have a huge impact on winning or losing a point, game, or match in tennis.

A doubles partner once shared with me that you have more time to get to a ball than you might think. Since then, if I keep this in mind, when I'm struggling to reach a short shot, running in as quickly as I can from the baseline, I tell myself, "I can get there, I have enough time." This simple positive thought almost always results in at least getting my racquet on the ball. Often, I'm able to send it back.

What's important is that I've not given up. Likewise, if I approach a shot with trepidation, my success rate is greatly diminished.

Belief is effective when learning a new tennis skill as well. One year, during the off season, I decided that I wanted to improve my lob consistency. I'd had trouble in the past, sending them too long and out of the court or too short, setting up my opponent for an easy overhead. But I knew that, with steady practice and perseverance, I could improve this shot. After about six months, I was able to reliably incorporate it into my match-play skill set. I never doubted myself. Once I had decided I would do it, I believed I could do it, and I did it.

Probably the most significant challenge to my self-belief was when I tested for my tennis instructor certification. It was one of the most demanding experiences I'd faced in my life. The intensity and pressure to perform shook my confidence. Though I prepared for my exam through study and on-court practice, self-doubt crept in. At one point, I even considered quitting. However, in the end, I stuck with it because my coach believed I could do it. Her faith in me bolstered my belief in myself and ultimately gave me the courage to do what needed to be done to complete the task.

Thoughts can have a tremendous impact on our performance. If you have constructive thoughts, believing you can do something difficult, you may experience a journey of self-discovery similar to mine. The power of belief may lead to greater success in your tennis game or perhaps elsewhere in your life. Tooth fairies may not be real, but make believe can remind us that our thoughts and beliefs can impact our commitment and ability, giving us the courage to do what we might have thought was impossible.

Communication
Revelation

Clear communication, especially when playing doubles, is essential for success during a tennis game.

Communication, between you and your partner and with the opposing team, is a key component in doubles match-play. Letting your opponents clearly know when a ball is out, or audibly announcing the score so that everyone on court can hear you, are important verbalizations to keep all players informed, especially when calls may be close or players lose track of the score.

In doubles tennis, partners need to learn to assess which of you should cover certain types of balls in situations that may seem ambiguous. Part of this skill includes verbalizing your intentions.

Then there are times between points when you should quietly confer with your partner regarding tactics or boost your partner's morale. In fact, I find that having a partner to talk to as the match progresses is one of the joys of doubles tennis.

During a Point: Deciding which partner should take a particular ball is actually a doubles skill that needs to be developed. Part of this skill is learning a way of speaking to communicate your intentions using concise words like *mine, yours,* and *switch* to convey meaning.

Whenever there is some question about who should take the shot, you will need to communicate early, quickly and clearly to establish which one of you will hit the ball. This is especially important in the case of lobs when the ball is traveling a bit slower and you have time to voice your intentions.

For example, if a lob is coming to the net player's side of the court, but it's too high for her to reach, as soon as she gets a read on this, she needs to shout to her partner "YOURS!" Her partner will then respond with "GOT IT, SWITCH," or if time is limited, just "SWITCH," and the two partners will switch sides of the court (ad to deuce, deuce to ad).

Sometimes, if a lob travels down the middle of the court and the net player shouts "YOURS," the baseline player may not have to run far from her home to reach the ball, so she should shout, "GOT IT, STAY" since her net player partner cannot see what is happening behind her and needs to know whether or not to switch sides of the court.

On a high ball over the net player, there may be times when the baseline player will shout "GOT IT, SWITCH" or "GOT IT STAY" before the net player has said "YOURS." This is good, but if the net player thinks that she can easily reach the high ball coming towards her, then she gets first dibs, even if her partner at the baseline has already told her "GOT IT."

However, the net player needs to be sure it's within her reach and execute her shot well if she is going to claim it. Beware that if she claims it, but then can't get her racquet on the ball, there is little time for the baseline player to back her up and take the shot.

When a ball passes between partners and it's not clear who's going to take the shot, if you're the player who is farther away from the net, you might say "GOT IT" or "MINE" if you feel you have a better setup for the shot. However, the player closer to the net still has first dibs on it, and it isn't necessary for her to voice this if she decides she's going to hit it.

If both players are playing from the baseline and the ball travels down the middle, it's more important for them to verbally establish who is going to hit it. Just remember that there is less time for talking when it's not a lob.

It's also good practice to shout "BOUNCE IT" if you think your partner is about to hit a ball that is going out of the court. If she lets it bounce, she will know whether or not to hit it. Be careful not to shout "OUT" before one of these balls crosses the boundary, because if the ball was in, you not only cause your partner some confusion, you may also affect the readiness of the other team.

Be cognizant that it's possible to overdo communication. Unnecessary communication can be a distraction to both of you and consequently weaken your responses. In general, try not to talk when your partner is about to hit the ball. If it's obvious whose ball it is, there's no need to say anything. Only say something during the point when needed. Practicing on-court communication will help you to develop a better sense of when to speak at the appropriate times.

Remember that you and your partner should only be vocal as the ball is coming towards you. Once you are sending the ball to your opponents, keep quiet, as it can be a distraction to the other team if you are speaking. Making a comment at the wrong time may not only annoy them, it might give them legitimate grounds for calling a hindrance.

Between Points: Communication is also important for partners between points, especially when you are the serving team. As the server, you may communicate a tactical plan for the serve, reminding your partner to anticipate a particular response from the returner. Sometimes you may simply want to say something positive and encouraging to your partner to ease her stress. Unlike communication during a point, communication between points is done quietly, out of earshot of your opponents.

Carefully choose what you say. The other day, I nearly reminded my partner that it was a match point before she served the next ball. But I stopped myself because I realized that it might add pressure or distract her. After we won the match, she told me that she had forgotten she was serving a match point. I was really glad I'd said nothing, as it may have derailed her focus.

All players are different, though, so tailor your comments to the person you're partnered with. Some people benefit from a bit of added pressure if they're reminded of the score and the significance of that particular point in the match. Others may crumble. Perhaps work this out before you play together for the first time to know which words of encouragement or focus work and which ones are detrimental for your partnership.

Non-verbal communication is another aspect to consider. When you are changing ends of the court between games, stick together with your partner. This body language is a reminder that you're there as a team. As my partner and I sit down to towel off and take a sip of water, we may exchange some strategy or simply try to help the other partner focus on something positive. Even if we say nothing, we maintain a connection simply by being together.

Also remember to walk with your partner as you change ends during a tie-break. You may want to exchange a few words of encouragement, but even if you're not talking, the non-verbal support of walking together makes for a stronger team.

With Opponents: There are important times for communicating with your opponents, especially at the beginning of the point when the score is announced. You may feel like your voice is easily heard, but unless you have increased your volume significantly, it is very likely the opponents will not hear you. Be courteous and shout the score to ensure everyone, including your partner, hears it.

That way, there is less confusion if you forget the score at the start of the next point, especially when you've had a long rally or switched sides of the court with your partner during the previous point. If more people can recall what the score was at the start of a point, it will be easier to retrace and identify where you are in the game.

It's also important to effectively communicate with the other players when you are calling a ball out. Don't delay and speak loudly enough so that everyone is clear the ball is no longer in play.

If you cannot increase your volume sufficiently, use hand signals to communicate your call. *Out* is signaled by pointing your index finger up in the air. *In* is signaled by waving your hands horizontally, like an umpire does in baseball when the player is safe on base. You can use your voice and hand signals at the same time, too, to ensure everyone knows the call; your partner may have her back to you and is relying on your voice to tell her if the ball is in or out.

Knowing the proper conventions of how and when to share information with your partner and opponents, about who should take the shot, what the score is, or when a ball lands out, is an important aspect of tennis that we must learn and practice, just like we do when learning technique and tactics.

Becoming adept at using clear communication will keep disputes at a minimum, enhance teamwork, and elevate your playing time on the tennis court. Like most things in life, tennis competition is a better experience for everyone when good communication is practiced.

Do You Mind?

Be mindful when you walk onto the court
and keep your thoughts focused on tennis.

Have you ever had a day where you're scattered in many different directions, then rushed to the tennis court to fit in your tennis match? Your mind is still stranded in the past where it's been processing the multitude of tasks for the day.

Next, it leaps into the future and starts enumerating the errands, meetings, or appointments you'll be attending following the match or planning what you're going to make for dinner that evening. It definitely isn't with you in the present moment, and you fail to focus on the tennis you've come to the court to play.

Focusing on the present moment is, of course, good practice throughout all aspects of life. In tennis, it's essential. There are many times in tennis when you must bring yourself back to the present and be focused on the moment at hand to stay in the point.

I begin this process when I arrive at the tennis court. I realize that tennis is a social sport, so of course I'm friendly and briefly chat with the people I've come to play with. But I'm prudent with this time, limiting it to five minutes or less while I unpack my equipment, take a sip of water, and prepare to go out onto the court.

Once on the court, I cease to engage in conversations. Instead, I bring my focus to the ball as I begin mini-tennis and stay focused during the entire warm-up. I believe that this is really important and has the potential to set me up for playing my best tennis. In my experience, when I do this, I play better right from the start.

Once the match begins, I'm focused on the ball, my court position, my opponents, and my tactical opportunities. The actual playing time is only about 17 percent of the total time players are on the tennis court. That means we should be acutely focused 17 percent of the time.

If we can focus our minds on one thing—such as watching the ball or moving our feet—while we're actually playing a point, we free up our bodies to respond to the game, based on what we've learned and practiced in previous training. Even though we are constantly making decisions during a point, they must be made automatically. A tennis point happens so quickly that there isn't time to weigh the pros and cons of a particular shot or think about details.

If you miss a shot, you have a quick few seconds to take stock. Have you ever realized your mind was completely elsewhere when you've missed? Don't dwell on it, but rein it back so you're focused and ready for the next shot.

Have you ever noticed the pros use a ritual as they prepare for the next point? It's the same every time. One of the most memorable is Rafael Nadal's pre-service routine. Using rituals before we begin a point helps to clear our minds and bring us to the present, so we can focus during the actual playing time.

During the remaining 83 percent of the match, we're between points and may need to catch our breath, speak with our partner about tactics, get a drink, towel off, change ends, flip the score card, and mentally assess our strategy, our successes and what's not working.

Be disciplined in between the points or when you're changing ends. If your mind begins to stray, bring it back to the present and to the reason you're standing there on the tennis court. You owe this to yourself, and in doubles tennis, you also owe it to your partner to maintain focus.

Pay attention to what's happening on your court. If you notice your partner has become unfocused, help her to return to the mental game by speaking a few words about what your next tactic should be, like a suggestion about where to place the next serve.

Tennis presents many challenges: a moving ball, changing targets, your own body movement—sprinting, turning, shifting your weight, and swinging a racquet—to effectively strike the tennis ball, and your state of mind. Shot selection and ball placement also require your attention as you respond to whatever shots you receive from your opponents.

It's an understatement to say that all of this is a great deal for your brain to cope with; yet you do it! If you stay focused on what is happening in the moment, you might discover that this state of mind helps you play your best tennis.

Earth, Wind, and Fire

If you typically play tennis indoors, practice outside to get used to the variable elements. That way you will be prepared when you're invited to join an outdoor match.

If you live in a part of the country that experiences seasonal changes in weather, you may be fortunate to have a tennis facility that has both indoor and outdoor courts so that you may play year-round. If you're a snowbird, then you probably migrate to regions where tennis can be played outdoors at all times of the year.

During our long winters in Central New York, tennis can only be played indoors. Each spring, when we return to playing outside, I've found there's an adjustment period getting used to playing in a different environment.

One day early in the season, after playing indoors in the morning, I had a match outside a few hours later and experienced a stark contrast in my performance indoors versus outdoors. I was frustrated with my outdoor game and surprised at how differently I played.

On the other hand, I realized that my partner and opponents may have felt the same frustration since all four of us had to adapt to the same conditions. The sun was in our eyes and the wind kept blowing the ball sideways—variables that we do not have to contend with when playing indoors.

Playing outside can add another level of challenge to the game of tennis. Just when you think you've developed great consistency with your serve or your crosscourt rally, playing outdoors may cause you to feel like you've regressed. Don't let this shake your confidence. Recognize that most players feel like they play worse outdoors than indoors until they learn to manage the elements of nature. Eventually, with sufficient practice, they learn to capitalize on these different conditions.

Outdoor variables can be categorized into three groups:

- earth, including the different playing surfaces of hard court, grass, artificial turf, Har-Tru, and clay

- wind and all its forms

- and fire, especially blinding sun and hot temperatures

Individually or in combination, each can potentially affect your performance. Learn how to alter your game in response.

Earth: The type of court surfaces you play on may be dictated by climate. For this reason, you will encounter different surfaces in different regions of the world.

I was visiting my parents in Kansas where I met a tennis pro from Australia. His favorite surface to play on was clay. He lamented the fact that there were no clay courts in Kansas because the winds are too strong and would remove the clay surface, requiring frequent and expensive replenishment. Hard tennis courts are the most common type in this area of the country.

Playing surfaces vary from hard court to clay or imitation clay to grass or artificial grass, a surface new to me that I encountered in New Zealand. Each of these will have a different effect on your game. Balls perform vastly differently when bouncing off these various surfaces, and some of these surfaces can significantly change over the course of a match, a day, or a week. It's good to gain experience on as many playing surfaces as you encounter so you can know what to expect and can add versatility to your tennis skills.

Wind: This element can be frustrating, especially when you're not used to dealing with it. When you go on the court on a windy day, immediately take note of its direction and strength, and remind yourself which way the wind is blowing every time you change ends of the court.

When the wind is in your face (hitting against the wind), hit groundstrokes higher and with more pace to get your shots over the net with depth. Without a lot of extra power, a ball that normally lands deep will land shorter, right in the strike zone of your opponent. Lobbing into a headwind can be effective, though you'll need to hit harder than you think to combat the effects of the wind.

Likewise, when the wind is at your back (hitting with the wind), hit your groundstrokes lower over the net and with more topspin to keep them in the court. Note that hitting with the wind may cause your normally consistent serve to land long. Over adjusting in response, you may find that you're not getting the second serve over the net because you've restrained your power too much. Wind from behind can also create havoc with lobs, sending most of them out of the court.

Crosswinds impact directional control. Hitting crosscourt may turn into hitting down the line as the wind carries the ball straight to the strike zone of the opposing net player. Alternatively, the wind may push your crosscourt shot over the sideline. Aiming over the net strap and keeping the ball low can help your groundstrokes stay in the court until you've got a feel for the wind.

Practice with your friends in the wind whenever you have the opportunity in order to develop the skills and experience to adjust your game to different wind conditions. Rest assured, with practice, patience, and a game plan, you can make the wind your friends.

Fire: Serving into the sun can have a huge impact on consistency. Practice serving into the sun at different times of the day as it moves across the sky. Additionally, it's helpful to learn the underhand serve for occasions when you repeatedly double fault because you're blinded by the sun. Even higher levels of players resort to this serve at times.

If your team includes a left hander, organize things so the left-handed player serves on the sunny side in the afternoon and the right-handed player serves on the sunny side in the morning.

Aside from the variables that affect the performance of the ball, it's also important to remember that outdoor elements can take a toll on your stamina and hydration. The heat of the sun, in particular, should be proactively managed.

- Choose a time of day to play when the sun is lower in the sky.
- Drink plenty of water, possibly with the addition of electrolytes, even before you go out on the court to play on a hot day.
- Wear a hat, sunglasses, and sunscreen to protect your body from the powerful rays of the sun. White or light-colored clothing will help reflect the sun and keep you cooler.
- Bring a wet towel onto the court to help cool your body during the time you're changing ends of the court.
- Shelter in the shade on changeovers if possible.

You can also learn to use earth, wind, and fire to your tactical advantage.

- It can be very effective to send a lob to an opponent who's facing the sun.
- If it's windy, keeping the ball low may ensure it will stay in the court and help you to outlast your opponent in a point.
- When playing on grass or clay, send balls into the short court. They won't travel as high or as far after bouncing, and if your opponent isn't quick enough, she may not reach the ball before the second bounce.

Tennis is primarily an outdoor sport, so embrace the extra factors you cannot control. Learn to respond to them or to use them in a way that gives you a competitive advantage when playing outdoors. The difference between you and your opponent may simply boil down to experience on the outdoor court. If you haven't played much outdoors and your opponent has, then she may have the advantage, knowing how to make the adjustments necessary to execute her shots well in spite of suboptimal conditions.

I encourage you to play outdoors frequently enough that you learn how to cope with these variables and develop a feel for making the adjustments required. Like anything we try to master in tennis, practice is essential. If you're well prepared, you can expand your tennis opportunities and get even more enjoyment from this game.

Above all, don't take things too seriously. If you let yourself relax, you might even get a few laughs from the unexpected bounce of the ball, the crazy way the wind can carry a ball, or your complete miss of an overhead when the sun is in your eyes.

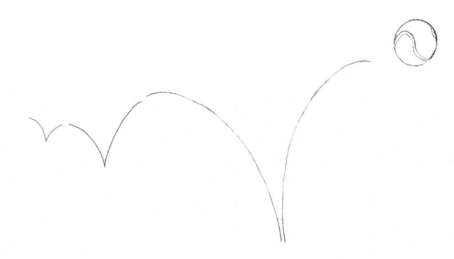

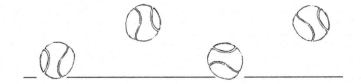

Eenie, Meenie Minie, Moe

*Be strategic when choosing which partner will receive
the last serve at deuce when scoring no-ad.*

If you're a recreational player, you probably play using the regular scoring system, in which you must win two successive points in a row to win a game that is tied at 40-40 (deuce). You've also probably experienced a game going on seemingly forever. This scoring system can be quite time-consuming and extend the length of tennis matches significantly, especially when teams are evenly matched.

You may not be familiar with an alternative to conventional scoring, called no-ad scoring, that's used to accelerate matches when playing time is limited. This means when the score reaches deuce, the next point is the game point and determines the winner of that game.

A key aspect of this format is that it's the responsibility of the server, at deuce, to ask the opponents which one of them would like to receive the serve. When the score reaches 40-40, the receiving team has a few seconds to decide who will return the serve, and that partner should raise her hand and perhaps say, "I'll take it."

four players have to be alert and move into their starting positions as the
begin from either deuce or ad side. If the receiver playing the deuce side chooses
take the return, the deciding point is played with the server serving from the deuce side.
If the ad-side receiver takes the return, the point is played from the ad side.

For one of the groups that I coach, I use Fast4 Tennis, a format that employs shorter mini sets that end when the first team wins four games and uses no-ad scoring. I chose this because it allows for more rotations with different partners against different opponents and gets players used to pressure but in a friendly atmosphere.

I have noticed that many players feel awkward when the receiving team needs to choose which partner will return the serve at 40-40. They tend to choose randomly, as though it doesn't matter who receives, because they don't want to offend their doubles partner by stating their preference to take the return.

In fact, this is not a time to tiptoe around feelings nor should one feel offended if her partner says she would like to receive. The choice of receivers should be made strategically and understood to be an opportunity to win the game.

Therefore, consider choosing the combination of receiver and receiver's partner that will most likely result in a successful and challenging return of serve. Here are a few things to consider when making this decision:

- Has one of you been more successful than the other with returns of serve during that game? If an obvious difference exists, choose the partner who has done a better job.

- Are you a stronger receiving team when player A is at the baseline and player B is at net or vice versa? In other words, does one of you play better at net with solid volleys and quick reaction times, and the other is better at the baseline with groundstrokes and placement? If you've noticed a difference, choose whichever setup is the strongest.

- Has the server struggled more when serving to one side of the court than the other during that game? If so, the receiving team should choose to receive from the server's weaker side of the court.

- Is server's partner a more active poacher on one side of the court? If yes, choose the setup which places her on her weaker side of the court.

You should definitely talk with your partner about how you'll make the decision as to which of you will receive the serve when the score reaches deuce *before* you start a no-ad match. It's OK to be competitive and choose which player will receive according to which choice will provide the best outcome.

Don't be shy. Be strategic. Use the guidelines above to decide whether you or your partner should receive the serve when using no-ad scoring. In addition to winning more points, such assessment of various aspects of the game may sharpen your awareness of winning tactics.

(For more details about scoring, see my discussion in Court Thought, "What's Love Got to Do With It?.")

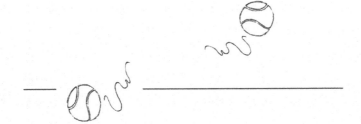

Energizer Bunny

*Manage your on-court energy by finding a balance
that puts your body in its best playing mode.*

Once when attending a high-intensity drill, I became frustrated with my poorly executed shots. I was playing against challenging players who were pretty hard-hitters, but it was nothing I couldn't handle in the past.

I tried adjusting my placement and my power but gained nothing. More often, my shot would end up in the net, go long, or travel right into the strike zone of my opponent.

Was it my timing? Was it my form? Was it my focus? Why was I not able to hit the ball well and win more points?

The longer this went on, the more frustrated I became. I also noticed I was very tense. My frustration and determination to perform better had gripped my whole body.

Instead of freely swinging my racquet, my body had tightened up, and I was muscling the ball. Once I took deep breaths to relax myself, my shots improved, and I became an equal contender to my opponents.

What does it mean to manage your energy on the court? It means to stay calm and loose when you feel nervous energy begin to grip you. At the other end of the spectrum, it can also mean to rev up your engine when you feel a bit sluggish in order to keep up with the pace of the game.

It's a fine line between being too revved up and too relaxed. Stay sharp but stay calm. There's a lot you can do between points to calm down or rev up, but let's focus on what we can do *within* the point itself.

Each player will need to find her own unique recipe to manage an appropriate level of energy. If you're overly excited and tense, as I was in the high-intensity drill, a good approach is to relax between shots.

This brief time between sending and receiving the ball is called the *centering moment* of the shot cycle, and when deliberately used to reset your state of readiness, can result in better performance on the tennis court. (See my discussion in Court Thought, "Slowing Down Time" for more about the centering moment.)

Nervous energy or frustration may cause you to tense up. Before the point even begins, use your slow, conscious breath to relax your muscles and calm yourself. During the point, use breath again to relax through your swing. This will help you to achieve an effortless ground-stroke with good ball control. Many players feel the need to load up their arms with power and muscle the ball instead of letting their racquet do the work.

Your body performs better and uses less energy when the muscles are in a stretchy elastic state. When muscles are tense, they're not as effective transferring the energy from the body to the racquet. The racquet head doesn't build up as much speed, so the power delivered at impact is diminished compared to the power from a relaxed swing.

If you find you are muscling the ball, take a deep breath and relax as you center yourself for the next shot. As you take the racquet back, think *relax*. Exhale through the shot to maintain loose muscles as you swing the racquet through the hitting zone. Recover, take another breath, and repeat.

The time for this is very short, but it's adequate if you recover right after you hit the ball, before it bounces on the opponents' end of the court. Doing this will help release the built up tension and help you reset yourself for the next shot.

Sometimes, a point develops into a rapid-fire exchange of the ball between players at net. I have noticed that each shot ramps up the excitement and creates tension in my body. If I can remember to exhale as I recover, I'm more able to maintain a supple body that reacts more quickly.

The next time you are faced with a frustrating situation on the court that creates tension in your body, use breath and the centering moment to reset yourself. Preparedness for each shot boils down to achieving a balanced state of readiness, especially when you feel under pressure. Practice using breath, both on and off the court. You may find that like many things in tennis, breath can be effective in other areas of life, especially when you are bombarded by stress inducers.

Every Breath You Take

Use your breath to modify your tennis performance.

I have to laugh when I'm in a lesson and a coach tells me, "Remember to breathe." I think to myself, "Why wouldn't I breathe? Breath is essential for life. My body wouldn't let me NOT breathe. So why am I being coached to breathe?"

However, they've noticed something I've not been aware of. My focus and concentration on the drill I'm performing has made me tense up to the point where my breaths are shallow and perhaps irregular. As a result, I'm not in my ideal performance state.

I usually smile or laugh when I'm reminded to breathe. This action relaxes me and gets me back to a more balanced state. Then I consciously take a few deep breaths and return to normal, at least for a while. Sometimes I go through this cycle a few times, with helpful reminders from my coach along the way, during an intense practice session.

The first time my coach drew awareness to my breath, I was surprised how closely linked breathing was to better performance. The breath softened my body; my muscles became supple and elastic. Less effort was required to execute my shots, and my technique improved. Balls sailed to their targets with power and control. Tennis felt easier.

Breath, though a basic bodily function, is both simple and powerful. You can use breath as I did to remove tension from the body. In her book, coach and author Gyata Stormon expands on the use of breath in different phases of the shot cycle (Stormon, 2019). Not only has Gyata played tennis for more than 40 years and coached for 20, she also practices and teaches yoga, which gives her an in-depth perspective on connecting breath to movement and mindset.

In her model of the shot cycle, Gyata advises players to use breath in the receiving and sending phases by inhaling as you take your racquet back, then exhaling as you hit the ball. Breath may help you to add power to your groundstrokes and crispness to your volleys. It may also help to provide the sensation that time during a point is elongated, and that you have the time you need to get to a ball, set up, hit, and recover before the next cycle begins.

Breath is also good to use before serving. If you feel uptight, after a double fault, take a few deep breaths, decide on your target and the type of serve you intend to deliver, then focus on your serving routine. This disciplined approach to setting up for serve should help you shave off errors and have greater success executing challenging serves to your opponents.

Breath can be used between points, most notably when you're feeling nervous. If you practice using breath as one of your habits to calm yourself, this will come more naturally when under pressure while playing in a match.

My lesson group was coached to develop a routine between points where we turn our backs to our opponents, breathe from the belly, and ground our senses by touching our strings or racquet dampener or consciously sensing our feet touching the court. This routine can be relied on as a reboot when your focus is falling off or thoughts of being down in a set loom large in your mind.

The next time you feel tense while playing, check in with yourself and use breath to reset. Like me, you may find this reminder amusing at first, but once you deliberately engage in this practice, you may be astonished at how powerful this simple function can be for your tennis game.

Focal or Vocal?

*Reserve your social chats for times before or after the warm-up
and match to minimize distractions on court,
stay focused on the game, and play your best tennis.*

Many of us think we can multitask, and some people seemingly do this better than others. We certainly multitask in tennis while bombarded with an array of rapidly changing situations such as judging the ball, selecting the shot, setting up for the shot, hitting, recovering, watching the ball, watching our opponents, and preparing for the next response.

It's a lot of information for our minds to track and process. Moreover, most of these tasks happen within microseconds. The more focused we can be, the better the responses we will make, and the better we will play.

It's important to remember that, when it comes down to it, multitasking isn't really giving our attention to multiple tasks or thoughts at the same time. It is actually shifting our attention from one task or thought to another and then to another in a short interval of time. During any single moment of this interval, our consciousness is focused on a single thought or task. It's virtually impossible for our brains to focus on two or more things at once.

Therefore, it's important to minimize distractions when you're on the court. An additional stimulus like having a conversation can hijack our attention. For example, in warm-up or practice, some players rally and talk simultaneously. I struggle in this situation as my brain battles to cope with these two points of focus, and my tennis suffers. Therefore, when I go out on the court to warm up, I don't talk. If a friendly player tries to draw me into conversation, I admit to them that I cannot talk and play.

I recognize that tennis is a social sport. Being with friends on the tennis court is one of the appealing aspects of playing. However, as tennis players, we should recognize that there are times when socializing is appropriate and times when socializing should be discouraged for the sake of the game.

The time for social chat is best reserved for periods before and after the tennis match—not attempted between points, between games, between sets, or during the 10-minute warm-up. Even if you can warm up and talk at the same time, be aware that your playing partner may find this difficult, and the other players on court, or even on an adjacent court, may find this distracting. The warm-up is our time to engage our eyes on the ball, feel the swing of the racquet, and move our feet around the court to sharpen our minds and warm up our bodies.

Respecting the warm-up and its importance is not only a courtesy to the other players, it may help you to start the match more prepared. You might not be aware of your own limitations until you discover that being focused in the warm-up actually benefits your performance in the first game of the match.

Remember, too, that if you're talking to the other players at the net before you go out on the court to play or after your match has finished, your voice may carry to the other courts, affecting those players. Make it your practice to have an awareness of others who are playing and be disciplined, restricting your socializing to the appropriate times. If you're determined to keep your mind on the game, you may find that you help to create an atmosphere on the court where everyone will play the best tennis.

Follow Through

Finish your swings, both forehand and backhand, with a follow-through.

The next time you're out on the court, do some warm-up swings with your racquet and no ball. Most likely, you will swing freely from the takeback to a complete follow-through.

Once you're warming up with the ball, pay attention to the follow-through phase of the swing. Are you still completing your swing? Does your racquet take a path across your body, or does it stop soon after making contact with the ball?

It's common for players to shy away from a full swing, especially during the mini-tennis portion of the warm-up. Players often feel that they will overpower the ball if they finish with a full follow-through.

However, a follow-through actually helps to control the ball and keep it in the court. To power down for mini-tennis, the takeback can be shortened, and the swing can be slower, but the follow-through should remain complete. Executing a full follow-through during the warm-up activates the muscles you'll use in the game, and it also reminds the brain to finish the stroke, which you'll need to do once you're playing.

The definition of follow-through is "The act of continuing something to completion." A quality groundstroke must be completed with a follow-through—generally up over your shoulder to generate topspin or down and out to execute a slice—to achieve consistency. (Depending on the situation, follow-throughs can also be across the body or on the same side.)

If you continue the swing after impact, the racquet gains momentum at the point of ball contact. An accelerating racquet can also generate increased spin on the ball, with the type of spin depending upon the direction of the swing path (low to high or high to low). Thus, a completed swing generates speed and control; the accelerating racquet head will transfer speed to the ball, and the spin will control the behavior of the ball. In the case of topspin, a good follow-through will cause the ball to dip back down into the court allowing you to hit with more pace and still keep the ball in.

I often observe players holding back, abbreviating their swing and finishing their strokes by stopping the racquet right after impact. They are afraid they will send the ball out of the court if they complete a full swing.

Much to the contrary, if you stop the swing right after your racquet hits the ball, the racquet will be decelerating at impact, which in turn decreases the spin you put on the ball, causing you to lose control. Consequently, balls will often go long and out of the court.

Stopping the racquet before the follow-through also causes stress on the forearm, as the delicate extensor muscles have to work to slow the momentum. Therefore, allowing a full, smooth follow-through will actually help you avoid overuse injuries such as tennis elbow.

When I'm coaching players to follow through, sometimes they have trouble letting go. They briefly pause their swing right after their racquet impacts the ball, and then they execute what I call an *afterthought follow-through* that is not part of the stroke at all, but really a separate action detached from their swing. This hesitation after impact, followed by a contrived finish up over the shoulder, results in no effect on the ball.

If you have trouble making the follow-through a natural part of your stroke, here are a few tricks to help you succeed:

- For the topspin follow-through on a forehand groundstroke, you can place your non-racquet hand up above your shoulder with your arm bent. Grab the racquet as it comes through the swing up to the shoulder area.

- For the two-handed backhand groundstroke, use a cue word to remind yourself to follow through. When you are setting up for the shot, think *up* so that you send your racquet up over your shoulder after impact.

- Other cue words like *out*, *reach*, and *stretch* can be used to help you remember the follow-through on a slice backhand groundstroke.

- One way to train a good follow-through motion is to practice with foam balls on a mini-tennis court. Caress the ball with a smooth stroke and follow-through rather than whacking at it. Be playful and have fun. Work on hitting with an arched, rainbow-shaped path that shows you are generating topspin.

Follow-through, though it occurs after impact, is part of the entire swing path. If you skip it, then the part of your swing occuring at impact will be affected. Your swing should be a single unit of motion from the time you drop your racquet after take back, move through the hitting zone, and finish with a follow-through. A complete swing will apply the optimal spin and force to the ball during the microseconds the racquet is in contact.

It may feel like you're hitting the ball harder and risking sending it long, but in fact, a follow-through will help to keep the ball in the court. Make follow-through a part of your complete swing to increase your consistency as well as to generate spin on the ball that makes it challenging to your opponents. Not only will your shots be more impressive, you will probably find this technique helps you to win more points.

From Chaos
to Consistency

*Consistency is key; keep the ball in the court and make fewer errors to win
the point.*

One of the main differences between higher-level and lower-level players is consistency, that is, consistently hitting a solid shot to keep the ball in play or to score a point. The first step toward developing consistency is to have the correct mindset, which is an openness to using the suggestions that follow.

This may mean giving up excess power and flashy winners that cannot be executed consistently, despite the excitement you may derive from them. Recognize that consistency isn't glamorous, but it's effective. If you're willing to open the door to consistency (and ultimately winning more), read on.

Consistency can be developed through practice and experience. There are several factors that contribute to consistency: eyes on the ball, contact point, and hitting to the correct targets, to name a few. Focusing on these during practice can help you to improve your ball control and change court chaos into consistency.

Keeping your eyes on the ball through impact may sound obvious, but it's easy to get caught looking at your target as the ball arrives in your hitting zone. Taking your eyes off the ball at impact has a huge potential to create a *mis-hit* where the ball hits the racquet frame or spins off the strings and ricochets off in an unexpected direction far from the chosen target area. As you stand there perplexed at what just happened, it doesn't always occur to you that you weren't watching the ball.

Though basic, keeping your eyes on the ball can't be stressed enough to beginner and intermediate level players as one important avenue to improving consistency. Several things can help with this:

- Plan your target before the ball comes to you. Think, "If it comes to my backhand, I will hit it to X. If it comes to my forehand I will hit it to Y."

- Take a last look at the opponent's end of the court as the ball crosses the net moving towards you. Note where the open court is and think about what shot you will use to send the ball there. Then transfer your gaze from the target to the ball and trust that you will send the ball to the chosen target without having to look at the target while you hit. This may sound like too many things to think about in the fractions of seconds to which you are limited, but you really can do this, especially with practice. In fact, lots of practice should make it automatic so you don't have to think about anything at that moment of impact.

- Remember that keeping your eyes on the ball also applies to serves. Think about and visualize serve placement before you serve, then keep your eye on the ball all the way from the ball toss through impact. Recover quickly and prepare to receive the return of serve with your focus on the incoming ball.

- Impact the ball out in front of you where you have better sight of it, especially with volleys. If the ball comes too close to your body, alongside you or above you, it is much harder to watch it impact the center of your strings. Volleys come fast so keep your feet moving and be ready to respond quickly as you watch the ball coming towards you.

Hitting the ball out in front of you is a technique that applies to nearly all shots—ground-strokes, volleys, overheads, and serves. Since you turn sideways to the net as you set up, out in front actually means in front and off to the side a bit.

Again, this simple advice sounds basic, but we often let the ball come too close to our bodies before we strike it. I ask my students to imagine the ball is radioactive, so they should hit it before it gets too close to their bodies. Creating space between you and the ball and making contact out in front helps your body to hit the ball with greater ease and natural form, resulting in good execution of your strokes.

- One way to develop a feeling for the optimal contact point is to self-feed groundstrokes. Stand behind the baseline, sideways to the net, drop the ball 45 degrees out in front of you with an outstretched arm, and reach out for it as you hit. Practice this until you have developed a feeling for creating the right space.

- Then go out with a practice partner or ball machine and aim to contact the ball when it reaches the same hitting zone. Remember to create space between you and the ball, moving your feet as needed. Make note of what this feels like. Similar practice can be followed when you work on volleys.

- The aid of video is helpful during this practice as it will provide definitive feedback as to whether or not you are achieving your practice goals.

Eventually you will develop a feel for judging the ball, moving your feet to position yourself in the correct location as you set up to hit your groundstroke or volley. Your hitting zone should be the same comfortable distance out in front just like you practiced with the self-feed. Focused practice will help this new habit become automatic.

Selecting higher-percentage targets will give you a margin of error, thereby increasing your chances of keeping the ball in the court and improving your consistency.

- One way to achieve this is to aim no wider than the singles sidelines when you send the ball crosscourt. This might mean that your ball lands in the alley some of the time, which is fine. But, if you aim for the alley and don't have good placement, then you're more likely to send the ball out of the court.

- When sending a lob, aim for a target about five feet inside the baseline. Don't aim deeper than that or the ball is more likely to bounce beyond the baseline while you are developing ball control and consistency.

- With volleys, aim for the "T" where the center line intersects the service line. This is a safe target because it's in the middle of the court, and it is less likely your ball will go out if you aim there. Plus, the T is a good target because it's difficult for the opposition to return a ball that lands near or on the T.

- If you want to volley at an angle toward the outside of the court, aim to the side Ts, where the service line intersects with the singles sidelines. This is a riskier shot than the T in the middle of the court, but it's still safer than aiming at the alley.

Developing good ball control leads to increased consistency in tennis. To acquire these skills and make them habits, focus on specific skills, one at a time, during your practice. Consistency isn't something that is easily quantified but, over time and in combination with improved court positioning, you will find you are leaving chaos behind, playing better tennis, and rising to a higher level.

fly
~~eye~~ on the ball

From San Juan to Yukon

Make the best of a suboptimal situation when not all four doubles players show up to the court. You can still have fun and improve your game with two or three players!

Best-laid plans don't always work out. Sometimes life gets in the way, and a doubles foursome has to figure out what to do when one player has to cancel at the last minute or forgets to show up. Rather than leaving the court without playing, the remaining three players have the option to stay and play alternative games.

A popular game for three is Canadian Doubles (also known as Australian Doubles). In this game, there's a doubles end of the court and a singles end. Players on the doubles end begin the point in the typical formation with one player at the baseline and the other at net. The singles player serves from a singles serving position near the center mark.

The doubles team must hit the ball within the singles sidelines of their opponent's court. The singles player is not restricted and may hit anywhere into the doubles court.

As you can imagine, the singles player is subject to a good workout if she hits the ball wide, opening up angles for her opponents. If she wants to minimize her running, her tactic should be to hit the ball to the center of the court, narrowing the potential angles of return. This game is lots of fun, easy to set up, and each player takes a turn on the singles end.

However, if you don't feel up to the running required to cover the entire singles court, or if you really want to practice your doubles game, you have the option to play another three-player version of doubles tennis that coach Gyata Stormon created when she was on holiday in Puerto Rico (Stormon, 2019).

Her goal was to create a three-person game that made tactical sense, as opposed to the game described above where the singles player is hitting into the doubles court, and the doubles players are hitting into the singles court. The beauty of Puerto Rican Doubles is that all three players get to use shots and hit angles that are normally used when playing doubles.

As a player who's interested in improving my doubles play during the time I spend on the court, my choice is Puerto Rican. It gives me the opportunity to use the doubles tennis tactics I've learned in my training. It's also a very good way to focus on consistency because the onus is on the doubles team to keep the ball in the lone player's side of the court. In addition, it's versatile enough that I can practice various doubles serving formations to keep the game interesting and challenging.

Puerto Rican doubles is set up in the traditional doubles formation on one end of the court with a baseline player and a net player. At the other end of the court, the lone player plays at the typical doubles baseline starting position with a *ghost* partner at net. The lone player covers one side of the court from the center line to the doubles sideline (ad-side or deuce-side) just as she would in regular doubles tennis. She has the freedom to send the ball anywhere into her opponents' end of the court.

To keep things fair, the two doubles partners can only hit into the half of the court that the lone player occupies for that point. This means the net player always sends the volley straight, and the baseline player always sends the ball crosscourt. If the ball lands in the half of the court where the ghost partner is imagined to be, it is out and the lone player wins the point.

It helps to place a row of drop-down markers, extending the center line between the two service boxes to the center mark at the baseline. This clearly divides the court into two halves and makes line calls in this area easier. If you're playing on a Har-Tru or clay court, you can simply draw a line with your foot to create this boundary.

Both Puerto Rican Doubles and Canadian Doubles proceed as typical doubles games with the server alternating between the deuce and ad sides. Players rotate after an agreed number of games so that they each experience all three positions.

In Canadian Doubles, players typically rotate after each set, whereas in Australian Doubles (its fraternal twin), players rotate positions after every game, and the singles player always serves. Feel free to use the rotation and scoring system that works for you, or create your own if you find something that works better for your particular threesome.

Sometimes, only two players are available to play. If these players prefer playing doubles instead of singles, they can play Ghost Doubles, a game played crosscourt between two players who start near the baseline as server and receiver.

They each have a ghost partner at net. If the ball lands on the ghost side of the court, it's out. Again, it's helpful to place a row of flat markers between the center service line and the center mark to clearly define the boundary areas.

Ghost doubles is a good way to develop consistency with your crosscourt strokes, both groundstrokes and volleys. To avoid being lobbed when you are drawn in on a short ball, be careful not to come in too close to the net. When moving into net, making your home just inside the service line is a good location until the opportunity arises for you to move forward and put the ball away.

These games are good, not only when short of players, but as training drills to help players practice certain skills. Next time someone can't get a sub to cover for them, suggest to the group that you still have options to play that are both fun and designed to improve your tennis skills.

Get a Grip

Check your grip. Are you using the appropriate grip for the position you are playing and the stroke you are executing?

It is always a stark reminder when one of the players attending my drills or coaching sessions reveals they have no idea what grip they are using, and further, that they had no previous instruction about grip. Grip isn't something many coaches teach. Thankfully, when I was beginning tennis, my coach made a point to teach us the correct grip to use for particular shots (serve, volley, forehand groundstroke, backhand groundstroke).

However, even though I'd been taught correctly, I actively decided to put my court thoughts about grip on hold because my brain was already focused on judging the ball, setting up to the ball, the follow-through, and other priorities. Remembering to change my grip for different shots was one more court thought I felt I couldn't accommodate at that time. I figured I'd make do with one grip and not worry about it.

Using the continental grip for everything seemed like a simple solution. Besides, grip probably wasn't that important in the scheme of things for a beginner. Maybe down the road when I was a 3.5 and wanted to generate more topspin, I'd revisit the topic.

Several months later, when I was struggling with consistency, I discovered grip had a much greater impact on the quality of my strokes than I'd anticipated. I realized that I couldn't avoid grip change and make further progress on my tennis journey. I had to pause to face the music and work hard to make grip change part of the fundamentals I employed in my tennis game. Once I took the time to do this, my groundstrokes improved dramatically.

Grip is an important aspect of tennis. It is a basic element that can have a big impact on your consistency. Most recreational players use three primary grips: Continental, Eastern Forehand, and Eastern Backhand.

Continental Grip is used for the ready position during your centering moment, for volleys (both forehand and backhand), for the dominant hand of the two-handed backhand, slice backhand, and for the serve.

Eastern Forehand and Eastern Backhand are used for forehand groundstrokes and one-handed backhand topspin groundstrokes.

Learn what these grips are and how to hold your racquet accordingly. Practice changing from one grip to another as needed for a particular shot. Using the correct grip will help you keep groundstroke balls in the court and help you send your volleys over the net with a better chance for scoring the point. The correct grip will help you add spin to your serve. So get a grip—the right grip—and win more points in tennis.

Get Back!

Don't be a spectator on the court. Recover immediately after hitting the ball.

Have you ever been caught admiring a shot you've executed well, perhaps one that had been difficult to reach? Inside your head, you're celebrating, feeling like you're a pretty darn good tennis player.

But then the shot is returned, and you're not ready to receive it. Maybe you respond too late, and the ball spins out of the court. You just lost the point, when, a few seconds before, you had already won the point in your mind.

The same might happen if you hit the ball poorly and stand waiting to see if it lands in the court. The opponent is ready to strike when your shot lands and sends it whizzing past you. Because you spent your recovery time watching and judging your own shot, you failed to prepare to receive the next one, and your opponent celebrates the point.

Don't be a spectator watching your own shots land. Your opponent will let you know if your shot is out.

Use the time immediately after you hit to get back to your correct home and assume that every ball will be returned by your opponent. You'll be better prepared to reach your opponent's next shot and win many more points if you incorporate this mindset into your game.

Your home is the optimal place on the court to receive the next shot. After you hit the ball, you should recover to the correct home where you briefly pause, making a small bounce on the balls of your feet (called the *split step*) as your opponent hits the ball.

As the baseline player, you have a choice between two potential homes. Recover to one by the time your opponent hits the ball.

- The majority of the time, your ideal home is just behind the baseline, not inside it. This places you back far enough to return deep balls.

- Occasionally, you may receive a short ball that draws you into the *transition zone* (the area between the baseline and service line, also known as *no-man's land*). The correct response is to move in to hit the ball and recover to the closest home, either back to the home just behind the baseline, or forward to your home just in front of the service line to join your partner at net.

- When you're receiving a serve that is often short, you'll likely want to start the point in the transition zone. This is fine, but it's imperative to recover to your correct home, either just behind the baseline or just in front of the service line, pausing and centering yourself before the opponent hits the ball.

- When you hit the ball from within the transition zone, immediately recover to your correct home after you hit. If you stay in the transition zone to receive the next shot, the ball may bounce at your feet and make it difficult to respond with a good shot.

As the server, it's important to recover after you serve. The return of serve often comes back quickly or at a tricky angle.

Consider these variables:

- Serve and recover to your home behind the baseline so you can stay in the point and hopefully create an opportunity for your partner to score.

- If you are playing an alternative formation like Australian, you will be serving from the singles serving position. After you complete your service motions, you'll need to immediately recover toward the baseline home on the side you have agreed to cover.

- If you serve and volley, it's unlikely you'll make it all the way to your home inside the service box before your opponent hits the ball. In this instance, be sure to pause and split step just before the opponent returns your serve even if it means you are standing in the transition zone.

  If the return goes to your partner, continue moving forward to recover at your correct home inside the service box as soon as you see your partner's taking the shot. If the return comes to you, recover to your home in the service box immediately after you've hit the ball.

As the net player, it's even more important to recover quickly to your correct home, because response times for each shot are shorter.

- When you've hit the ball, recover to the net player home approximately in the middle of the service box, keeping your eyes on the ball while you assume your ready position. If you've recovered to the correct spot, you'll be both ready and well-placed to move to the ball to defend the alley or poach a middle ball.

- If you blunder when poaching and accidentally hit directly to the opposite net player, don't give up by assuming the point is over. Drop the judgment about your shot and scurry back to the home where you came from as quickly as humanly possible to give yourself a chance to salvage the point.

Playing from the baseline or the net, it's very common to lose track of your bearings as a point goes on, especially if you've had to move around the court or change sides with your partner. If you find you're missing shots, take a minute to assess where you were on the court when you made the mistake. Were you at or near the correct home, or had you recovered to the wrong place before you hit?

Recovery is often overlooked by players. Strive to make it a part of your practice. If you can be mindful of moving toward your correct home after each shot, you'll set yourself up for a more effective response. Move to the ball, execute your shot, and get back to your home as quickly as you can to be ready for whatever comes next. Once recovery becomes ingrained as part of your game, you'll find you're responding more quickly and hitting better shots which will ultimately lead to winning more points.

(For more about homes, see my discussion in Court Thought, "No Place Like Home.")

Gratitude Attitude

*Play with happiness. Don't let frustrations with your performance blind you
to why you are playing in the first place.*

Not long ago, I was on court feeling tired, a bit sore, and not thrilled to be with some hardcore players I didn't have fun playing in the past. Every shot felt like an obligation rather than a privilege, and every mistake became a frustration. Needless to say, I didn't play well that day.

In hindsight, I could have played much better. It was all about the attitude I had brought with me on the court that day. I had forgotten the joy, the gratitude, and the fun that had originally lured me to tennis.

A few days later, I had the opportunity to watch some top high school and college tennis players during their practice session. Their shots were exquisite and their agility amazing, but something was definitely missing. There were no smiles, no words of encouragement amongst themselves, and no apparent enthusiasm. There was no energy, no positive vibe, and no excitement amongst these players. Where was the joy?

I was certainly envious and admiring of their tennis skills, but I realized as I watched these young people that it was possible I have more fun playing tennis than they do. Sadly, they may be traveling down the road to burnout if the feeling of joy has left their game.

The next time I was on court, I remembered to pack my gratitude attitude in my tennis bag. I remembered to feel glad and appreciative to be there. When I made a mistake, I thought of it as a challenge and a chance to improve, which helped me to hit the next shot better.

A positive attitude gave me permission to make mistakes without focusing on the negativity. As a result, I felt happy and played better.

When you hit a bad shot, I suggest you shake it off quickly and move on. If you dwell on it, you won't be ready for whatever happens next. One bad shot can lead to another if you don't learn the art of leaving your mistakes behind you. Moving on gives you a better chance of returning to the present moment, being centered and ready to respond to the next shot that your opponent sends.

In doubles, I frequently hear "sorry" between partners on the court, especially in cases where they haven't played together before. Consider avoiding apologies except in rare circumstances. Apologizing for missing a shot not only wastes your energy, it keeps you dwelling on the mistake and elicits an unnecessary response from your partner that may distract her from the game.

The partner knows the mistake was not deliberate. Make an agreement ahead of time to withhold your apologies so you can both move on to the next moment, unencumbered. Instead, offer each other positive encouragement, or say nothing.

Most points in tennis end in someone's mistake, but there are usually several shots preceding the final shot that can be celebrated. Focus on these successes for a better mental game and greater enjoyment of your tennis match. Sometimes the errors we make are quite funny; let yourself have a laugh when they happen. A smile will help to reduce nervous tension which, in turn, helps you move on to the next point more ready and relaxed.

We all have off days on the tennis court. If you can remember to pause during one of these times and remember why you love tennis, you'll leave the court feeling better than if you'd let your mistakes loom large. With a gratitude attitude, your off day may take a different route and even become a great day.

Tennis happiness can be the catalyst that brings us to the court each time we play. Without it, we may as well stay home. Remember to let yourself feel the joy from your successes, however small they may seem.

Sometimes it even feels good to celebrate with your opponent when they hit a remarkable shot. Doing this breaks down barriers with the other players and creates a pleasant vibe for everyone. Sharing the smiles, the laughter, and the camaraderie will make your tennis experience a better one and fill your cup with gratitude for the opportunity to be on the tennis court.

Inside Out

Focus inward when practicing, outward when playing.

Experiences demand your attention in different ways. When you're driving, for example, you watch the road, staying alert for hazards and opportunities to keep safe and get to your destination. Your mind is looking outward as you take in information and respond to it.

By contrast, when you're reading, you block out the world around you and keep your inward focus on the printed content to efficiently glean and process information. When you play tennis, sometimes your focus is inward, and sometimes it must be outward. How do you choose when to do what?

During practice, your court thoughts will be more inwardly focused, mainly on technique. During play, your court thoughts will be outwardly focused on tactics and your opponents. Be mindful of this distinction.

For example, if you're practicing a specific technique to improve your backhand, your focus should be inward. It may be on your setup to the ball, adjusting your position so the ball is in the sweet spot of your strike zone. You may be judging where to move in relation to the ball bounce. Do your best to block out external distractions.

If you find your attention is dwindling, pause what you're doing and actively bring it back to the court thought you're working on. When you're deeply in the zone, thinking about your objective, developing a feel for the execution, and moving with a rhythmic pace, one ball after the next, you may perceive a kind of meditative state. This focused state of mind is excellent for efficient learning.

However, if you do this when playing a match, you'll find it's difficult to maintain a simultaneous awareness of the activity around you; seeing the open court or preparing to defend a shot becomes especially challenging.

During play, focus on the opponent. You may still be inwardly focused between points, but once the ball is in play, your focus should expand to the opponent's end of the court. Assess tactical opportunities regarding your position on the court and placement of the ball as well as defensive tactics, anticipating where to be to cover your end of the court.

Outward focus relies on trusting your tennis habits to take over so you can observe your opponents and play competitive tennis. You must believe that your practice sessions have provided you with the skills you need to play the game, and you must let your body react and use them.

That's why we practice, to create habits we can fall back on when playing. During match play, if we're bogged down in thoughts about technique or whether we're winning or losing, we'll not be keeping a clear mind that's ready for whatever comes our way.

You may find your focus shifts to a technical court thought because you've missed a shot. When the point is over, execute a few ghost swings to remind yourself of the correct technique, then turn your focus back to your opponents, trusting that your body will remember how to hit the shot.

It may be more effective to assess where you were on the court when you missed the shot rather than thinking about correcting your technique. Being in the right place on the court can have a greater impact on your game than having perfect technique. Save your technical work for practice time.

During a point, keep thinking to a minimum and trust your body to react as you trained it to do. The time for thinking in a match is between points. Assess your situation and make a plan.

An appropriate court thought for match play would be, "Watch my net player opponent. If she moves toward the middle to poach, be ready to send the ball down the line." Once the point has begun, let yourself respond to the situation that transpires.

Experienced players will find this easier to do than players still learning the skills of tennis. As you develop better technique and begin to trust your skills, you'll start to see the open court on the opponent's side of the net.

I remember the first few times it happened for me. It was as though a veil was lifted, and I found I was seeing more of the match than just the ball hitting my strings. At first it happened intermittently, as though the veil would lift, then fall, and I'd be back to my inward focus. Over time, I was able to see my opponents more and more.

You still need to watch the ball as it comes towards you and when you're hitting it, but as soon as you hit, recover and watch the opponents. The quicker you recover, the more you'll be able to observe, and the more you'll be ready for their response.

When serving, you'll be inwardly focused as you prepare yourself during your serve ritual. Once you've served, recover quickly and be ready for your opponent's return. At this point, your focus will have changed to an outward perspective. Likewise, in the other three starting positions— receiver, server's partner, and receiver's partner—you want to be present in your body and ready to do your job after the point begins.

Whether in practice or play, be mindful of the circumstances for inward and outward focus on the court and use the perspective that's appropriate for the situation. When playing a match, you may be tempted to fix a technique, but don't let your thoughts stray. Keep your focus on the game and park your desire to assess your technique until your next practice session.

Laid-Back Dude

Be sure your wrist is laid back for a one-handed backhand groundstroke. It's the strongest, most stable position and results in better performance while reducing the risk of injuries.

If you feel pain when executing a tennis stroke, your body may be telling you something about your technique. Pay attention.

Not only will repeated stress cause injury, but continuing to ignore proper technique may also stall your progress to better performance. If you seek help before the pain becomes chronic, then correcting your technique should make the pain go away and simultaneously improve your game.

Tennis elbow, medically known as lateral epicondylitis, is a very common injury. It's caused by overstressing the tendons that run along the extensor side of the forearm (the hairy side) and anchor into the elbow. Proper technique helps to protect this potential hotspot, but it's easy for a beginning player to forget about that while they focus on other aspects of learning the game.

Tennis elbow manifests as a tenderness on the outer point of the elbow joint. If left unchecked, the pain may escalate. Recovery can take months of rest, icing, and physical therapy.

When it happened to me, I couldn't face the prospect of a long hiatus off the court while my injury recovered, so I learned to play left-handed for a while. That experience actually taught me some new things about tennis technique that I was able to use later on when I returned to using my right hand. Though the few months I spent playing left-handed had value, I wished I could have avoided this detour in the first place and identified the cause of my tennis elbow before it reached a level of disabling severity.

When I learned to play tennis, my natural preference for executing a backhand groundstroke had been to play one-handed. Though using a two-handed backhand is more common, the one-handed stroke felt freer to me, so I stuck with it.

Without realizing it, I failed to lay my wrist back—a technique that helps to protect the elbow. In addition to playing more than I probably should have been because I loved the game so much, I continued to ignore the discomfort. This was a poor choice.

When I inadvertently had my racquet restrung too tightly, the inflammation that had been slowly building became severely debilitating, seemingly overnight. Eventually, I had to withdraw from playing, which was a devastating setback in my tennis journey.

When the wrist is fully laid back, it has more strength and helps to absorb the shock of the impact, thus protecting the elbow. If a player drops her wrist when hitting one-handed backhand groundstrokes, tennis elbow often results over time. Dropping the wrist removes the shock absorber, so the full force of impact directly assaults the tendons leading to the elbow joint.

Rest, icing, and sometimes a cortisone injection will help to eliminate the inflammation, but unless the cause is dealt with, your tennis elbow will likely return. Take the time to sort out your technique. Have a coach assess and advise you to help you fix the problem. Use focused practice to learn the new technique, but be patient and don't overplay. Being overzealous could cause another setback. Over time, with dedication, your new technique will be assimilated, and the tennis elbow will heal.

Recognize that the process to correct your technique will take time and patience. A new way of hitting the ball may feel awkward and frustrating. Your timing and setup may be messed up. That's OK. Give yourself permission to make mistakes.

Focusing on a new technique will require an adjustment period. Don't expect perfection, don't judge yourself, and welcome the challenge. In my case, my coach helped me to retrain my one-handed backhand and also develop a two-handed backhand, which was an awesome stroke to learn for generating topspin and power.

Both approaches were effective in preventing me from relapsing. I still use a one-handed backhand in certain situations, but it's nice to have two backhand choices in my arsenal of strokes. I'm happy to say I haven't suffered from tennis elbow again, and my new technique for the one-handed backhand has improved my consistency for that stroke, so I'm actually playing better tennis.

> To check that your wrist is in extension, or laid back, start with the hand and forearm in a straight line. Then, move the back of the hand toward the hairy side of the arm. This is extension. For one-handed backhand groundstrokes, an extended wrist will result in your thumb pointing up and back towards the body.

Laughter Is the Best Medicine

Laugh off your mistakes.

We've probably all heard the adage, "Laughter is the best medicine." We feel better after laughing. It releases positive energy, washes away stress, and we're told it even exercises our internal organs. People who laugh more lead happier lives.

Last week, I indulged myself by taking a tennis lesson followed by two tennis drills. For some reason that day, I was in a more forgiving mood and had a lighter heart. When I made mistakes on the court, whether it was a ball bouncing funny or my shot going in a ridiculous direction, I found that many of them amused me. Instead of feeling frustrated, I found myself laughing in response.

The laughter had a profound effect on my performance. It prevented negativity from creeping in and kept me from dwelling on the mistake. I've certainly noticed how being angry with myself about one point in a game can spill into the next. Laughing also helped to relax me and keep my muscles supple.

On this day, however, my laughter seemed to release any disappointment I might have had over losing the previous point. As a result, I was ready and focused for the next shot, which I usually executed well. Sometimes my next shot was extraordinary!

The effect of the positive outcomes created an emotional feedback loop which perpetuated more good tennis. After three and a half hours on the court, I reflected I'd played my best tennis ever that day.

Psychology professor Dr. Peter Scales, tennis coach and author of *Mental and Emotional Training for Tennis*, encourages us not to take ourselves too seriously on the court. In an interview with Ian Westermann, he shared that he once had a coach tell him, "You're not good enough to be that upset." (Westermann, 2019).

When I was laughing at my mistakes, I thought about how we rarely see professional tennis players laugh off their mistakes, but we often see them get angry at themselves. It's too bad.

So all this being said, my court thought for you is to laugh at your mistakes, lighten your heart, and permit yourself to enjoy the game more. If you do, you may be amazed at how well you play.

Listen to Your Body

Listen to your body and don't overplay to the point that you risk injury.
Balance on-court and off-court activities to improve your tennis skills.

The lure of improving quickly tempts many new players to the point of overexerting their bodies. I went down this path when I was a beginner, but I developed severe tennis elbow and soon discovered how much injury will set you back.

It can be hard to resist the temptation to spend lots of time practicing and playing to make yourself a better player. Sometimes you want to spend more time on the court to continue working on skills, even when you start to feel discomfort in an elbow, shoulder, wrist, or knee. Some believe you should just push through pain. But take heed and listen to your body, especially when you feel a bit of pain; allow yourself to recover by resting.

The good news is that not all efforts to improve your game must be done on the court. There are options available for practicing off court that you can mix into your training to help you avoid overplaying.

Don't wait until your body starts to hurt. Learn to balance on-court and off-court activities for making steady progress in your tennis game and minimize the risk of overuse injuries. If managed well, you can still practice lots of repetitions by mixing off-court practice with your on-court regime of lessons, drills, and games.

Below is a list of suggested off-court activities that you can do to facilitate your tennis practice without stressing your body.

- Serve practice: Practice your ball toss off court. Fifty to 100 times per day can greatly improve your serve consistency. You do not need to be on the tennis court to practice this.

- Ghost swings: Practice swinging your racquet each day, with forehand, backhand, both groundstrokes and volleys. Move through the swing slowly and deliberately, assessing the angle of the racquet face, the cock of your wrist, the position of your elbow, the impact point (position of imaginary ball), the shift of your weight through the swing, etc.

  Gradually speed up the swing until the last 10 or more swings are at full racquet-head speed. If you can do this in front of a mirror (a dark window will do if you don't have a big enough mirror), even better.

- Video analysis: Take videos of you or of you and your doubles partner playing or practicing. All you need is a tripod and your phone or iPad to do this. Instead of practicing on court two successive days, use the next day to analyze the video to see where improvements can be made or where improvements are working.

  Depending on what we're working on, video can be used to analyze our strokes (technique) and/or how we're playing the game (tactics). We often think we are doing something correctly, but without watching, there is no way to confirm this. Don't be shy. Watching a video of yourself gives valuable feedback.

- Watch YouTube videos: Find YouTube videos of others playing, whether it is a specific lesson online (like serves from Feel Tennis or a video about lobs from Essential Tennis) or video from the professional matches (like highlights of the U.S. Open men's final) that makes its way onto YouTube. Watching others play tennis can actually improve your own game.

Be specific about what you are analyzing. For example, watch the player's recovery positions after hitting a shot, or watch a serve play that wins a point.

- Read a tennis book: There are many books you can read regarding tennis. My favorite is Gyata Stormon's *On the Ball: Doubles Tennis Tactics for Recreational Players*, which breaks down doubles play into manageable units for all positions on the court. It is filled with diagrams that make her narrative very easy to follow and understand.

  Full disclosure: Gyata is my coach, and I was the tennis content editor for *On the Ball*. I read it through six times as it was being written, and each time just reading it, it noticeably improved my game!

  There are also books about getting a handle on the mental game, which is a huge challenge in tennis. So many shots can be affected by our thoughts. Confidence or self-doubt can make you win or lose a point. Learn how to optimize your positive focus and discard the negative gremlins that like to linger. This can help you to find more joy in tennis as well as improve your performance.

  Most recently, I've read Peter Scales' *Mental and Emotional Training for Tennis*, which covers a wide range of topics for the mind. Another good book is *The Best Tennis of Your Life: 50 Mental Strategies for Fearless Performance* by Jeff Greenwald. You can digest it in small bites and in whatever order appeals most to you at the time.

- Physical fitness training: Spend time off the court building your stamina with aerobic exercise to improve cardiovascular efficiency. Practice a fitness regime that tones, stretches, and strengthens muscles needed for quick movement on the court. If you're lucky, you may find a trainer who understands tennis and can help you specifically improve your strength and agility on the court.

- Yoga: My tennis coach is a huge advocate of yoga. After years of intense training and competition to the point where her body hurt, she discovered that yoga was the perfect off-court activity for tennis players. It teaches you to breathe better and builds strength, flexibility, and balance. It also improves patience and the ability to focus in challenging situations, both attributes needed on the tennis court.

It may take some experimenting to find a style and teacher that suits you best. Don't be discouraged if you don't like your first class.

- • Socialize: If tennis is social for you, then why not spend time with your tennis friends off court? Go out for coffee or have lunch together and talk tennis. Discuss things you experienced on court, or spend time planning a tennis event together.

Employ some of these ways to make improvements to your tennis game without actually being on the tennis court. Create a healthy balance between on- and off-court activities from the get-go, and you may avoid injury altogether while your game improves more quickly than you ever thought possible.

Make a Plan

Make a plan and stick to high-percentage tennis tactics when you play.

We're generally better off when we make a plan than if we approach a task without direction. Sure, it's fun to be spontaneous and unplanned occasionally, but if this is your standard operating procedure, you will probably find you don't often achieve the results you are seeking. I saw a bumper sticker that said, "A goal, without a plan, is just a wish."

Tennis is no different. *How* we approach the game will have an effect on the outcome. If we simply react to the ball, we may find we're playing defense more than offense. On the other hand, if we keep in mind the higher-percentage moves, we may find that we are the stronger offensive team.

High-percentage tennis refers to choosing shots that give you the best chance to keep the ball in play or to make a winner. This means using lower-risk shots, such as shots that land well within the lines of the court or cross the net at the lowest point, while still challenging the opponent with a degree of difficulty. Ultimately, they are shots that give you a higher success rate.

Some examples of high-percentage doubles include

- sending the ball to the other baseline player,
- avoiding the net player,
- keeping the ball low and deep,
- picking on the other team's weaknesses, and
- covering the court by occupying the right homes.

Making a plan and being deliberate at the beginning of a point, whether you are the server or receiver, will be more successful than hitting the ball randomly.

The earlier that tennis players connect technique to tactics, the sooner they will have the skills to execute more deliberate, challenging shots when under pressure. Beginners have short-term goals. Their plan is basically to make contact with the ball and get it over the net. There is little thought to placement.

And, if they're absorbed by technique, they will fail to see where their opponents are. Often, their pleasure comes from the newly acquired ability to partake in a ball exchange. When they're very new at tennis, they may even be amazed and amused that they can do this.

Novice players have moved just beyond this stage and have some tactical thoughts in mind. But because they're still learning technique, ball placement can be random much of the time. Often a winner is due to sheer luck, and they're grateful when they hit a shot that goes past the opponent and stays in the court.

Intermediate players have reached a point in their journey where their shots are more deliberate. Having trained and practiced more, they've learned that placement and power can make a difference between winning and losing the point, and they are usually able to control these two variables to some reasonable degree.

Many players at this level have developed consistency by choosing tactical low-risk shots and targets. Their game is considered high-percentage tennis, and they reap the benefits with a greater number of wins.

There are some players who have the skills for consistency, but they play more erratically. Too often, they are tempted by the allure of the more exciting high-risk shots. In the heat of the moment, they abandon high-percentage tennis and go for show, such as a down-the-line shot while on the run. These impulsive reactions will often lose points.

Players best prepare themselves on the court when they have a plan before the start of each point. The foundation of their plans should be rooted in high-percentage shots and targets. Having a plan also keeps players a bit sharper and gives them more time to react once the ball is in play because tactical choices have already been identified.

As receiver, I like to start the point with a couple of contingencies in mind. For instance, when I'm receiver on the ad side, if the ball comes to my backhand, I decide I will send it crosscourt to the backhand of the server.

If the ball comes to my forehand, and I'm faced with an aggressive poacher at net, I decide I will send the ball down the line using an inside-in shot. These two choices are in my mind before the point starts so that, once I'm in action, I already know what to do.

Talk between points to make a plan with your partner. Share your observations and together figure out responses that may weaken the opponents' offense. A good plan also means choosing targets that put your opponent on the defense, setting up your partner to score, and using the lower risk options to achieve these.

Occasionally, circumstances may put you in a situation where you are only left with a high-risk response, but when given a choice, a solid player chooses the safer play. It may not seem as glamorous, showy, or exciting, but high-percentage tennis will make you more successful. So get into the practice of making a plan and use the best options available to play better tennis.

there's no place like home...
there's no place
like home...
there's no place
like home...

No Place Like Home

Learn where to recover on the court after you hit.
These locations, called "homes", are the optimal areas from which you can
best respond to the next shot from your opponent.

I was born and raised in Kansas. Like many children, we looked forward to the annual broadcast of *The Wizard of Oz*, especially as we felt we could relate to Dorothy, who also lived in Kansas. Her famous words, "There's no place like home," resonated with me and have carried with me throughout my life.

When my tennis coach first introduced me to the concept of *homes* on the tennis court, I could hear this phrase echoing in my head. Dorothy's words continued to ring true as I discovered, through lessons and practice, how important homes were for playing effective doubles tennis. Of all the things I've learned in tennis, the consequence of being in the correct home on the court has had the greatest impact on the success of my game.

Your home is "the location on the court where you center yourself and get ready to receive a ball by the time the opposing player hits the ball," Stormon writes in *On the Ball: Doubles Tennis Tactics for Recreational Players*. This puts you in a place from which you can get to balls with relative ease, thereby increasing your chances of setting up well to hit the ball and score more points.

From these home locations, you have better coverage of your portion of the court, leaving fewer open court opportunities for your opponents. Additionally, when you are positioned at the correct baseline home, you can easily determine if a ball is going to land in or out of the court before you hit it.

Once you hit the ball, you should attempt to recover to your home (or as near to it as possible) before the ball bounces on the opponents' end of the court. Sometimes things are moving so quickly, especially if your opponents are at net, that you can't get back to your home in time. In this case, it's better to be centered and ready at the moment the opponent hits the ball than to be caught on the move, trying to scramble back to your home.

Recovery to the correct home is scientific, and I would further say, non-negotiable. If you are centered and doing a split step from your correct home when your opponent is hitting the ball, you have the best chance, THE BEST CHANCE, to hit the next shot well to keep the ball in play or win the point.

Different roles in doubles tennis require you to be located at different homes. Learning your correct home helps to define which partner covers which area of the court. The following discussion is about homes for the standard one-up and one-back formation in doubles.

Server's starting location and recovery to home: Your typical doubles serving location is about halfway between the center mark and the doubles sideline. Some players like to stand closer to the center mark. This can be helpful if you are trying to place a T serve. Other players like to stand closer to the doubles sideline, which allows you to serve with greater angle.

Wherever you choose to start the point, it's imperative to immediately recover to your home after serving the ball to play out the point. Your baseline home places you behind the baseline, your outside foot in line with the singles sideline or close to that. Sometimes your serving motion takes you into the court, so you will have to remember to move back behind the baseline when you recover. I like to incorporate recovery into my serving practice to reinforce this habit.

Receiver's starting location and recovery to home: It is common to stand inside the baseline to receive serve. If you do this, quickly recover to your home after returning serve—usually the baseline home where you center yourself—ready for the next shot.

Baseline home: As the baseline player, after you hit, immediately recover to your home behind the baseline. The exception is when you have to run in for a short ball. In this situation, there is usually not enough time to return back to the baseline home, so it is best to recover to your home just inside the service line.

From your baseline home, always let the ball bounce before hitting it. This allows you to accurately determine whether or not the opponent's ball will bounce in or out of the court.

Net player home: If you are playing at the net and your partner is at the baseline, you should be moving between two areas of the service box while the ball is being exchanged by your partner and the other baseline player.

> — Be at your *offensive home*, which is in the center of the service box when the ball is in front of you and has passed the opposing net player on its way to her partner. Your gaze point is on the ball and you should be ready to move forward from there to hit the ball if the opportunity arises.

> — Move to your *defensive home*, which is a few steps back from the center of the service box towards the T when the ball is behind you and your partner is preparing to hit. Your gaze point should be on the opposing net player, and if that net player looks like she is about to hit the ball, prepare to defend.

> Sometimes you may have time to back up a couple more steps, for example, if the opposing net player is hitting an overhead. The bottom line is to have ceased your movement and be ready and centered by the time the net player strikes the ball.

> If the opposing net player does not hit the ball, you should quickly move forward to your offensive home. Be centered and ready to intercept the crosscourt reply before the opposing baseline player hits the ball.

Playing both up at net: There are occasions where doubles partners are both up at net, such as when you, as the baseline player, have been drawn in to receive a short ball or have created an opportunity to join your partner at net by executing an approach shot. In this case, both you and your partner occupy homes at the net that are different from each other; your position is determined by the location of the ball on the opponent's end of the court. This is called the staggered-offense system (Stormon, 2019).

It is well worth your time to study and understand the correct homes; you will play better tennis and win more points. Note that where you stand to begin the point, your starting location, is not necessarily the same as your home once the point is under way. In these cases, you'll have to move to the home after the point has begun, as discussed above regarding serves, return of serve, and playing both up at net.

When you play, do your best to stay mindful of your court position relative to the correct home. Recognize there are slight variations to these homes based on the situation occurring as a point is played. When you've made a mistake or had a success, take stock of where you were when the point ended. Did you defend well or win the point because you were at the correct home?

Though I may not be in Kansas anymore, wherever I'm playing tennis, it always rings true that there really is "no place like home."

(For more information about the centering moment and recovery, see my discussions in Court Thought, "Slowing Down Time," and Court Thought, "Get Back," respectively.)

On the Line

*Do your best at making line calls
and assume your opponent is doing the same.*

Line calls in tennis can be contentious. In competition, most players feel greater pressure to win. A point, ending with a ball landing close to the line and difficult to judge in or out, might be generously awarded to a team by their opponents in a casual match. But when stakes are high in a formal match, such as a USTA competition, where a win-loss record determines what teams go on to play in post-season matches, that same opponent might be motivated to call that same ball out and take the point for her team.

My doubles partner and I have been frustrated in matches where our opponent questioned our line calls from her end of the court, despite the fact we were much closer to where the ball bounced. We've also felt annoyed when our serves that hit close to the center line and appeared *in* to us were called *out* by the opponent. Many times, you will hear players complain about the bad line calls their opponents have made.

Once, when listening to an Essential Tennis podcast about handling tennis cheaters (Westermann, 2018), I heard that for all the bad calls you feel were made against you, you've probably made an equal number of bad calls yourself without realizing it. What you think you saw isn't always what has actually occurred. In other words, you or your opponent weren't *deliberately* making bad calls, but your perception may not have been accurate.

It can be frustrating to play against opponents who frequently seem to make bad line calls. It can also be distracting to your game if you feel you were the victim of injustice. If you let it matter too much, getting stuck in negative thoughts can cost you your focus and impact your performance. It's possible some of your opponents' line calls were inaccurate. It's also possible they were correct, and it's you who was seeing through tinted glasses.

Our eyes and brains aren't as precise as we assume, and we're all prone to making mistakes. The bounce of a ball happens quickly, and sometimes we are not in the optimal position on the court to accurately judge whether it bounced in or out. But without linespeople, we must make our best stab at it.

To help you with your judgment about whether a ball was in or out, apply the following conventions:

- If you have any doubt at all about a ball being out—it looked like it might have been out, but you're not sure—then assume it was in and give the point to your opponent.

- On the other hand, if the ball is close but looks out, go with your gut and call it out. Some players are frightened to make a bad call and therefore don't stand up for what they feel to be true. Have the courage to call a ball out when you believe that's what you saw.

- If neither you nor your partner saw the ball, then consider it good, or, in this unusual case, you might ask your opponents to make the call.

- If you are in disagreement with your partner about a line call, the uncertainty means you should assume the ball was in and give the point to your opponent.

- If your partner was certain about a line call AND had the best view of it between you and her, and you saw it but weren't certain if it was in or out, then stay quiet and let your partner make the call.

- If the ball is on your opponents' side of the net, it is THEIR call, not yours. Unless they solicit your advice, do not give your opinion of whether a ball was in or out.

- If the ball in question is a serve sent by your partner, and you can see it was out, but the opponent did not call it out, then play it as a good ball. When you are the server's partner, never call a serve in or out.

- As soon as you see a ball land out on your side of the net, call it immediately. Don't wait until after you see the outcome of your shot. With that said, it is quite common, when playing on the baseline, to be hitting a ball that's close to the line while you are calling it out.

- If you're playing on har-tru or clay courts, it is completely acceptable to examine the mark the ball has left on the court to determine whether it was in or out, after the point is over and before making the call. Note that it is considered bad behavior to cross over to the other side of the net to look at the mark unless you are explicitly invited to do so by your opponent.

- If you can see a ball flying through the air that looks like it is going to land out, you must wait until it has either bounced out or crossed the baseline or sideline in the air before calling it out. Don't assume it is out until it is beyond the court. Some balls with enough topspin will actually dip in and not be out, even though they may appear to be sailing on a trajectory that would land outside the court.

If you think the ball is going to land out, what you CAN say to your partner, as the ball flies through the air, is "bounce it" or "watch it" to signal to her that it might land out and that she should be cautious about hitting it. But don't say, "It's going out," or "It's out," before it's crossed the line, as this may mislead your opponents if the rally ends up continuing.

- When you call a ball out, say it loudly enough for everyone to hear. In addition to your verbal call, you may opt to use hand signals for opponents who can see you but may not be able to hear your voice, especially if your back is turned away from them. The index finger pointed up signals *out*, while the full hand facing down signals *in*.

- When you call a ball out, say it with confidence. Do NOT say, "It was a bit out," or "I think it was out." You must be assertive, or you create uncertainty, inviting your opponent to doubt you and challenge your call. A ball is either in or out. It's that black and white. It's never a bit out.

Ball calls are not a time to worry about being overly polite or concerned about embarrassing someone or hurting their feelings. Just say, "out." Likewise, a ball that is 99 percent out is 100 percent in. That means, if it touches the line at all, it's in.

- If you find that your opponent seems to consistently make bad line calls, then on the third or fourth time, when you are pretty certain your ball was clearly in, you can ask the opponent, "Are you sure?" They may stick to, "Yes, it was out," but at least it puts them on notice that you are not going to put up with them being sloppy and potentially making bad calls. Hopefully they will be more careful from that point onwards.

- To improve your ability to make good line calls, learn which lines are easiest to see by each partner. When calling the serve, the service line is most clearly visible to the receiver's partner. As long as she has started on the service line, she should make this call.

The center line that divides the two service boxes is more clearly visible to the receiver, though the receiver's partner can give support and occasionally make the call. The outer sideline of the service box, which is actually the singles sideline, is more visible to the receiver, and she should make the call. When calling this line, give your opponent the extra benefit of the doubt. Your dislike of getting aced on an angled serve may cloud your judgment, and because the server's partner has a great view of this line, she will definitely know if you have made a bad call.

- Note that it is very difficult for you or your partner to clearly see the baseline on the opponents' end of the court. If you are questioning those calls, you are probably wasting your mental energy. If you're playing at the net, you do, however, have a good view of the sidelines and the center service line on the other end of the court, often an even better view than your opponents who are making the call. It's these lines that are more appropriate to question, should you feel the need to do so.

- After the point is in play, with respect to calls on the baseline and sidelines, there are other considerations. The baseline is usually most easily called by the player on the baseline. However, if her partner is at the net, she may glance back to help or even make the call at times. If the player on the baseline makes the call out and still hits the ball, the call *out* stands.

  This sequence is quite acceptable, because when a ball looks like it's going to be close, you have to get your racquet back and prepare to hit it. Your racquet may already be moving forward by the time you see where the ball landed. Finally, calls on the sidelines should be made by the player on that half of the court. The view of the partner looking across the court is poor.

Remember, the time you have is very short to both judge whether or not the ball is out and then to make the call. You must make split-second decisions. Learning, understanding, and practicing the conventions outlined here will improve your ability to make good calls. Remember that you, and most every other player, wants to win and intends to be fair.

If you feel your opponent makes a bad call, let it go so you can focus on the next point. If they are frequently making bad calls, say something, but don't dwell on it, or it may put you off your game. Respect your opponents and don't let it upset your rhythm if you are questioned about your line calls. Just aim to be more careful and move on. Most of the time, bad line calls are done in good faith and not as a deliberate cheat.

It's human nature to make mistakes. How you handle it says more about you than about the person who erred. There are times, in life, when it's worth standing up for yourself. By contrast, there are times when taking a stand isn't worth your energy, and it's better to dismiss the incident and move on. Sometimes there's only a small distinction between the two, and discerning the right action is equally prone to mistakes.

There's a difference between believing you are right and making sure everyone else knows it. Sometimes, you have to resist arguing with your opponent and instead, be satisfied that deep down, you believe you were right, and that's good enough. Holding on to anger can be self-destructive, and letting things go can be freeing.

Choose wisely as you navigate volatile situations. When you give someone the benefit of doubt and assume good intentions, you empower yourself to find more peace and greater happiness in life as well as on the tennis court. (For more information, see my discussion in Court Thought, "An Honest Mistake.")

One Court Thought at a Time

*When making changes to your game, focus on one court thought at a time
to streamline your practice sessions and derive the greatest benefits
from the time you invest.*

One of my favorite times of the year is the period directly following the USTA spring and summer seasons when I can integrate significant changes in my tennis game. Formal competition against unfamiliar players illuminates my strengths and weaknesses, helping me to identify new skills that I'd like to add to my toolbox. Making and prioritizing a list of focus points, or what I call *court thoughts*, prepares me to embark upon this loop of my tennis journey.

Learning requires inward focus and sufficient repetitions of the skills you seek to learn and master. This is why it's best to make major changes during the postseason, when you no longer have to keep your attention on your opponents and formal competitions. If you don't play in seasonal leagues, you have greater freedom to make changes at any time.

Lessons, drills, and practice matches will provide the best ingredients for transforming your tennis game (see my discussion in Court Thought, "Tennis Diet"). Whenever you decide to embrace change—whether it is tactical, technical, physical or mental—it's important to do so in a systematic way.

I'm a firm believer in focusing on one court thought at a time when making changes to my game. This means that, even when working on a particular stroke during my practice, I stay focused on a single aspect of that stroke: the take back, the follow through, the swing path, getting turned, the ball toss, or stepping into my shot, etc.

Once, as I practiced a volley drill with great intensity, my coach observed a tremendous amount of tension in my body. As you know, quicker reaction times are required when responding at the net. I was so absorbed in the aspects of timing, placement, or stepping into my shot that I had tensed up during the drill to the point where I wasn't steadily breathing.

She advised me to make a conscious effort to breathe to make my body more responsive. Keeping this court thought at the forefront of my mind, I put the other aspects of good volley execution on hold and clung to the single thought: breathe. To my surprise, focusing exclusively on the breath relaxed me, made my body more supple, and enabled me to smoothly execute the mechanics of the stroke.

Working on one court thought at a time is important, whether I'm the student or the coach. When teaching, I limit my instruction to one court thought to help my students identify and refine one aspect of the skill we're working on. I aim to keep things simple so that they don't feel overwhelmed with too much information. We need to be relaxed to play our best tennis while we drill a particular skill. Focusing on one thing at a time helps to minimize frustration and the tension that can result, thereby promoting an optimal learning state.

If we're working to improve volley skills, for example, we may initially discuss the entire sequence involved with hitting a volley from using the continental grip, holding the racquet high in ready position, getting turned, stepping into the shot, and hitting the ball out in front. In addition, we may rehearse a few sequences in slow motion (without the ball) to get a feel for executing the stroke.

Then, when we start our practice drill, I may remind them about the grip but after that ask them to focus only on getting turned before making contact with the ball. This means that they shouldn't be thinking about the other steps in the sequence. Although all of them are important for executing a good volley, it is best to focus on each component, one at a time.

Learning something new can be overwhelming and may even make you feel like a failure at times. Permit yourself to make mistakes and realize that, if you are focused on one thing, other aspects of that skill may be temporarily sacrificed during the learning process. You may even think you're getting worse before you start to feel you're getting better.

However, you may be more likely to stick with your training if you anticipate that you might feel awkward during the process. Eventually, your newly acquired skill will start to feel normal, and over time, you'll get better and better at it. Ultimately, your body will react and perform without your mind having to think through the action.

If you want to cover multiple things in your practice sessions, record them in your court notebook so you can systematically work through the list, one item at a time. Avoid cluttering your mind with multiple court thoughts in a given moment. The mental chaos will likely frustrate you, and jumping from one thing to another in a single practice session tends to result in little to no improvement in any of the things you dabbled in.

Allow yourself sufficient time to work on one aspect of a skill. When you've achieved a desired level of consistency, you're ready to move on to the next point of focus and follow the same protocol. Using a systematic approach, focusing on one court thought at a time, is a learning process that ensures quality practice and progress. This method may help you reach your goals sooner and give you a feeling of accomplishment as you travel along your tennis journey.

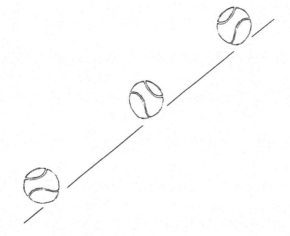

Pacemaker

As the server, it's your job to set the pace of the game. Be respectful of your opponents and the rules that govern timing between points, games, and sets.

A pacemaker, most of us recognize, is a medical device implanted in a person's chest to help the heart maintain a regular beat. Pacemaker is also the term for a lead runner who sets the initial pace of a long-distance run. In tennis, the server is considered the pacemaker, setting the pace of the game.

Servers generally set a reasonable pace, in my experience. However, I've also been on court with servers who rush and servers who delay. Rushing your opponents can be annoying, and there have been times when I've had to tell the server I wasn't ready and asked her to please wait. I find it equally irritating when a server delays the game by taking too long to serve. It breaks my rhythm and my focus.

In my opinion, tennis is more fun when all the players know and abide by the rules and etiquette that determine what happens between the points. Keep things running smoothly in a tennis match by following a few guidelines.

The server has control over the time between points with how quickly she serves a ball after a point has ended or how quickly she serves a second serve if she misses the first. Some servers may have faster rhythms than others.

For the sake of the overall enjoyment of all players, it's important that this pace is not too quick and allows ample time for the receiver and receiver's partner to set up. Nor should it be too slow and make all the players wait for the start of the point.

Some servers have an annoyingly long ritual before they launch the ball, and it's important for the receivers to have a strategy for handling the delay without losing their focus. Likewise, it is important for receiver and receiver's partner to keep up with the reasonable pace of the server.

When you are the server, use a steady rhythm between points to keep the game moving along, but don't rush your opponents. It's important you glance over to their end of the court to see if they're ready before you begin your serve ritual.

If you sense they are being deliberately slow, however, you can try to increase the pace by using body language. I've experienced the receiving team deliberately taking extra time before they indicate they're ready. It has been irritating at times, and in some cases, I've tossed the ball as though I'm going to serve to signal that I'm ready and waiting for them.

There is a tennis adage that states, "Always slow a losing game." This means that if you feel the match is getting away from you, slowing things down, especially before you prepare to serve, can help curb your opponents' momentum while you regain your focus.

However, don't slow things down to an annoyingly slow pace. Respect your opponents and keep the game friendly and fun.

As receiver, be a good sport and cooperate with the pace that the server has set. If you feel the server has rushed you, do not attempt to hit the ball. Let it go by you or catch it, then tell her you weren't ready and ask her to please take her serve again.

On the flip side, it's considered bad etiquette to intentionally slow things down as the receiving team. The receiving team must make the effort to move to their positions on the court in a timely fashion before the start of each point.

Beyond widely accepted etiquette, there are also specific rules that govern the game's pace within the overall time limit allowed. The USTA specifies the time permitted between points, games, and sets. All players should be aware of these times and make every effort to be compliant.

- Between points, players are allowed 20 seconds to move to their positions, set up, and start the point.

- At the end of even games, players are allowed 20 seconds to start the next game.

- At the end of odd games when players change ends of the court, with the exception of after the first game of a set, they are entitled to 90 seconds before the start of the next game. This time includes flipping the score card, rehydrating, and toweling off.

  Players usually sit down for some of this time, and doubles players often use this opportunity to encourage each other and talk about tactics. At the end of the first game, that is at 1-0 or 0-1, players may not sit down and must move to the other end of the court without delay.

- Between sets, players are allowed two minutes even when they don't change ends to start the next set.

The effort to keep games moving along includes efficiently managing the balls. After the warm-up, there should only be three game balls on the court. During play, stray balls should be retrieved in a timely fashion and at the appropriate moments. Balls should be returned to the server and server's partner.

The server needs two balls to start each point; therefore every player needs to have the capacity to hold an extra ball somewhere, either in a pocket, waistband, or tucked under the skirt. The server's partner usually holds the third ball for the server, though some servers prefer to start the point holding all three.

When a point is over, hustle to pick up and pocket a ball. If the server already has two balls, don't slow the pace of play by sending the third ball to the server or server's partner. Wait until the end of a point when there is time to quickly send it over to the serving team.

Resist hitting a let or a serve that is out; leave it to go out of bounds or grab it and pocket it if it lands nearby. If you try to retrieve it, your actions will delay the next serve unnecessarily, slowing the pace of play, and messing up the rhythm of the server.

Only pick up a ball if it presents a potential hazard on or close to the court. Otherwise, leave these balls until the end of the point when you can pick them up and return them to the serving team. Keeping balls recycled takes a bit of practice so that you become adept at doing it at the appropriate times. Once this becomes habit, you'll notice how much more smoothly the entire game flows.

When players follow these guidelines, everyone on the court benefits. You'll have a much better time when you're playing more and waiting less. Ultimately, a game that flows facilitates fun.

Patience Is a Virtue

Be patient with yourself when implementing technical changes to your game.

A while back, I was working on improving my volley technique, especially my timing. Many times during these drills, I felt way out of my comfort zone. Even so, I remained positive and patient with myself.

Slowly, but surely, after many repetitions, I began to notice changes in my responses. Without thinking, I began to consistently move forward to hit the ball out of the air, instead of waiting for it to come to me and letting it bounce. It was a moment for celebration.

Most of us want to be good at what we do. We see how something is done by experts who make tennis skills look easy. Then, when trying the skill ourselves, it becomes apparent that we have a long road ahead of us.

Some athletes quickly clip along the road to proficiency. Often, they are labeled as *naturals*. They may indeed be born with some measure of innate ability. They may also have had training in another sport which gives them a head start. Whatever the reason, they learn quickly and play well, and they are envied.

We all learn at different rates in different ways. Some of us seem to require fewer repetitions before we're competent. Others, like me, may require more practice, more analysis, and more repetitions to acquire a new skill and assimilate it into our repertoire. It may take hundreds of repetitions to learn something new and hundreds more to master it.

Don't worry if along the way, you feel like things are getting worse before they get better. Be patient.

Learning a new technical skill is best accomplished progressing through a series of steps. If you can add video feedback to any of these steps, it will accelerate your learning.

- Begin swinging your racquet without a ball. Shadow strokes (ghost swings) are ways to practice setting up for the shot and slowly moving your racquet through the path of the stroke. Repeat, gradually increasing your racquet head speed, until it feels natural.

- Self-feed groundstrokes or volleys. This will help you develop your skills hitting the ball without having to predict where it will bounce first. Self-feeding forehand strokes is easier than backhand strokes, but both are possible. Be patient adjusting to self-feeding the backhand. It helps to toss the ball up so you have more time before it bounces, allowing you to place both hands on the grip for a two-handed backhand.

- Rally with a practice partner or ball-machine to experience receiving the ball. This step adds practice in judging where the ball will be and moving to the right area on the court to hit the shot.

- Play for points. Keeping score often helps to keep you focused on good execution.

- At this point, you're probably ready to attend group drills which are usually designed as games that emphasize a particular tennis skill. This is a good setting to take risks. Give yourself permission to try out your new skill and make mistakes.

If you've followed the progression described above, you're ready to try using that new skill in a real game. Be patient with yourself if you revert to your old habit. If this happens, you may want to revisit a few of the practice steps before you play again.

It takes courage to leave your comfort zone. Persevere and be kind to yourself. Celebrate the small successes along the way. If you truly believe that a change will improve your tennis, what have you got to lose? In the long run, you'll come out the other end a better player.

Learning new skills happens in stages. Trust that working through this series of steps will eventually lead to good execution. Set goals and aim for reaching benchmarks along the way. Don't just covet the endpoint of mastery; enjoy the entire practice journey. Embracing the process will ensure that you won't take a detour down the road of burnout and frustration.

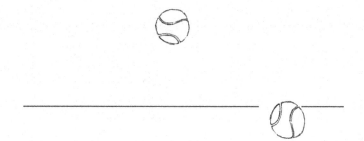

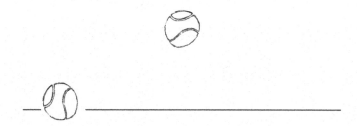

Practice with Purpose

Practice with a specific purpose in mind each time you go out to hit balls.

We're often told that practice makes perfect. However, this is not exactly true. I have found that practice can be a loose term amongst tennis players. In reality, meaningful practice isn't simply spending more time on the court. It should be purposeful and focused in order to make real improvements. Let me explain.

Many players believe that practice means going out and hitting lots of balls outside of game play. They think that the more balls they hit, the better they will become in their quest to improve quickly. When they don't reach their goals as soon as they expect to, they may be driven to spend more time on the court hitting more balls, aiming for quantity, not necessarily quality.

Unfortunately, this approach often leads to overuse injuries such as tennis elbow and not to improvement. What is often overlooked is that the approach you take with your practice affects the rate of improvement.

For example, if you practice with a ball machine, and your goal is to hit as many balls as you can so that they land in the court on the other side of the net, then that is what you will achieve. However, this approach won't help with the skills needed to win more points in a game.

You won't come away from that practice with better placement, which you will need in a game in order to avoid the opposing net player. And it won't teach you how to send a challenging ball to the opposing baseline player to weaken her response. So, how do you get more out of your time on the court?

Practicing with purpose—with a particular objective—is a way to enrich your practice and maximize the benefits. There are several things to consider: targets, tactics, technique, making a plan, and being deliberate.

For example, aim for specific targets whenever you're hitting balls. Make sure the target connects with a doubles tactic, such as avoiding the net player or forcing a weak return from the baseline player, deep or to the player's backhand.

If you're hitting balls on the ball machine or rallying with a practice partner to improve your topspin or backhand groundstrokes, add tactics to your technical practice by visualizing the opposing net player and avoid hitting your ball within her hypothetical reach.

Be deliberate with your shots. If you're hitting groundstrokes, focus on crosscourt targets deep into the far corner of the court. If you hit three in a row, aim crosscourt for the first two and down the line for the third. Don't hit randomly and then evaluate your shots saying, "Good, I sent two crosscourt and one straight." Be deliberate with each shot. Make a plan and execute it.

If you sent three shots, and two were crosscourt and one went straight, but only one went where you intended it to go, don't be satisfied. Use that feedback to focus more, adjust your technique, and try again to hit the intended target. The same process can be used for volleys, lobs, and serves.

Work on one aspect of a technique or tactic at a time. For example, with groundstrokes, you may choose to focus on topspin. Work on this until you begin to become proficient. Then choose another aspect to work on and practice that with sufficient repetitions. Perhaps limit your practice session to a maximum of one or two areas of improvement.

You may take several weeks to cover the various focus points sufficiently before moving on. But, if you are deliberate, you will progress more quickly than if you are random and undisciplined.

After you've seen improvement in your consistency and have successfully implemented the technical change into your game, it might be time to start experimenting with something new like a slice backhand or lobs. Follow a structured plan to master these skills as well.

When practicing serves, do this with purpose. Hit a succession of first serves, followed by second serves. Or alternate between a first and second serve. The goal is to follow a purposeful protocol. You might try for power with first serves and placement with second, or perhaps add in spin. (For more information about serves, see Court Thought, "Second Chances.")

Also include recovery after serving, that is, moving back behind the baseline after you serve. Practicing recovery as a part of the serving process will make it automatic for you in a real game. Practice serves from the doubles serving home or from the center mark. Practice standard recovery, or practice recovery for Australian serves or I-formation serves where players move across the court to a particular location after hitting the ball.

If you attend drills, it's easy to get caught up in the energy and excitement without keeping targets or technique in mind. To get more out of a drill, I like to make a plan in my head to focus on a specific stroke or particular target. This enriches the drill time for me, and I usually gain more from it.

Choose something to focus on during a particular session. It could be sending groundstrokes low over the net, executing a lob over the net player, or trying a passing shot down the alley every time a wide ball comes to you. When playing at net, push yourself to move towards the ball to catch it on your racquet before it bounces instead of letting it come to your feet or backing up and letting it bounce.

If you're up at the net with another player in a drill, you can practice staggered offense. The other player doesn't need to know what you're doing or join you in the practice of this particular court movement. What's important is that you are responding to the situation in regards to your own position on the court.

There are many ways to practice with purpose. When you're seeking to improve your tennis, design a plan that fits your objectives and carry it out. Avoid the mistake of hitting lots of balls without a practice goal or overwhelming yourself with multiple court thoughts. It will only frustrate you, and your practice session will result in little to no improvement.

By contrast, when you practice with purpose, one focus point at a time, you will spend your practice time more efficiently, get more out of each session, and make improvements to your game more quickly. Enriching your practice time will help to advance you along your tennis journey, and it may give you a frequent sense of achievement with each incremental improvement.

Profile Your Opponent

*Take full advantage of your warm-up and get a read on your opponent
before the match starts.*

Going onto the court for a match, especially when playing against strangers, you're probably wondering what you're up against. What are the opponents' strengths and weaknesses? Is anyone a lefty? Can they move quickly on the court?

The unknown can ramp up our anxiety and impact our performance. I've felt nervous excitement when asked to sub in a doubles group I haven't previously played with or in a USTA match as I face new opponents. But as soon as we start hitting, the first few minutes on the court begin to reveal things about my opponents that are both tactically useful and helpful in displacing my fear.

One way to get a read on your opponents is to observe them during the standard 10-minute warm-up—including mini tennis, groundstrokes from the baseline, volleys, overheads, and serves—before the match begins. Be sure to share what you've learned with your doubles partner in the few moments after the warm-up and before the match begins.

Make mental notes:

- Does she have a powerful drive from the baseline?
- Does she use slice?
- Are her volleys weak?
- How consistent is she keeping the ball in play?
- What's her serve like?

Test your opponent by sending balls to her forehand and backhand, both groundstrokes and volleys:

- Does she avoid her backhand?
- Does she move well on the court?
- Does she seem to have good ball control?

Your opponents won't always reveal their strengths during the warm-up; they may prefer to wait until the actual game begins to employ some of their tricks for a surprise effect. Therefore, be alert to how a player's game may change once the match begins. Take the opportunity to share further observations with your partner as the match progresses.

You should also be aware that sometimes a player will have beautiful groundstrokes during the warm-up that are surprisingly ineffective during a match. By contrast, I've made the mistake of judging a player to be in the beginner range of the spectrum because her strokes were unconventional or seemingly unpolished, and yet during the match, she was a fierce and effective competitor able to use these skills to win lots of points. But, despite these various caveats, the warm-up is a good time to obtain a basic profile of who you're about to play.

Serves, usually a minimum of three on each side of the court for each player, are an important part of the warm-up. This gives our shoulders a warm-up and instills confidence that we can get our serves in the service box, even when we may be a bit nervous. It is also an opportunity to check out our opponents' serves so we have a better idea of what to expect during the match.

- Is it a fast serve?
- Does she use spin?
- Is she consistent?
- Does she seem to have a favorite spot to place her serve?

Unfortunately, in friendly matches, many players are in a rush to start the game, and after they warm up groundstrokes and volleys, they choose to skip the serve warm-up and opt for *first ball in* (FBI) instead. That means each player gets as many attempts as needed the first time they serve.

In my experience, players like having the option to use FBI because they feel it takes the pressure off of their first serves. But the deficit of warm-up serves could put you at a disadvantage. You may get your first serve in on both sides of the court on the first try, but when you serve the third point, you may double fault, having had only two serves up to that point instead of eight (six from the warm-up plus one for each of the two points served).

In a USTA match, serves are a standard part of the warm-up. In a friendly match, when I'm playing with people who prefer FBI, I propose a compromise where everyone warms up serves (three balls per side) AND we play FBI. That way, everyone gets what they want.

Use the warm-up as an opportunity to profile your opponents and gain what advantage you can. The more information you have about your opponents, the sooner you can know what tactics might help you to dominate or defend in the match. Gaining control and winning the early games in the first set can give you momentum from which your opponents may never recover.

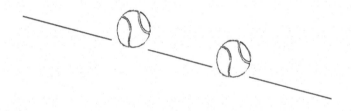

Second Chances

Develop a second serve and make it conservative yet challenging.

Have you ever felt like you're facing the firing squad as you prepare to receive serve? You've already seen the server blast the ball at your partner. Now it's your turn, and you know it's coming like a bullet.

Serves can be intimidating. I've stood on the court and watched the serve whizzing its way towards me with so much speed and power that I'm lucky to get a racquet on it.

However, I've often found that only a low percentage of these balls actually land in. Most are long and bounce beyond the service line. The server has opted for intimidation and power at the expense of accuracy.

The next thing that happens is usually predictable: Either the server opts for control on the second serve and is exceedingly cautious—making it easy to return—or she blasts the second serve much like the first. Rarely does it succeed.

If you're this player, strengthen your service game by developing a second serve that is less risky yet challenging. Work to develop two distinctly different serves for each attempt, a first serve and a second serve, to avoid double faulting and maintain the advantage as the serving team.

We are freer to take more risk with a first serve. Therefore, most players apply more power to a first serve at the risk of accuracy. What most players don't know is that, in doubles, it's recommended you make about 75 percent of your first serves.

Think about it. This means you should only miss one or two first serves each game. Ideally, you want your second serve to be 100 percent successful, so a more conservative approach is advised.

Your opponents will expect this and try to capitalize on a weaker second serve to win the point. It's easier for them to approach the net or lob off a weaker serve.

Therefore, be strategic with the second serve. Keeping a serve deep, as well as developing placement and spin, can make it more difficult to return and can be used for both first and second serves.

Controlling the placement of the serve keeps it challenging. Consider serving to the opponent's backhand; for many players, this is their weaker side. Wide angled serves can be effective, too, though the server should be prepared to run in for a short, wide return, which is the most common response to an angled serve.

I often choose to place a body serve for my second serve. Placing a serve directly towards the opponent's body can be effective because it forces the opponent to make a quick decision to move. If they don't move to the side quickly enough, the ball will be too close to their body and jam up their stroke. Placing a body serve also increases the chance of the serve landing in because this middle target is farther away from the side boundaries of the service box.

To practice serve placement, divide the service box into two target areas using drop-down lines that run from the net to the service line. Practice these targets on both sides of the court.

Once you are proficient, deliberately placing the ball in either half, divide the service box into three areas: A, B and C for *alley or angled* (toward the outside of the service box in the direction of the alley), *body* (to the middle of the service box), and *center* (down the middle of the court towards the T), respectively. Remember to practice on both sides of the court.

Spin serves are effective and challenging second serves. Developing spin on your serve pulls the ball down, and therefore makes your serve more consistent. Spin helps to catch the receiver off guard and force an error. There are a few types of spin serves, with the slice serve being the first and easiest to learn. It can be a wise investment to take some lessons to learn how to execute them.

Occasionally, throw in a soft or short second serve, especially if you've mainly been hitting deep second serves. This might catch your opponent by surprise, as she may have to rush in towards the net to reach the ball in time. The receiver may also overpower a softer serve and send her return out of the court because she's anticipating a serve with greater velocity.

Develop an array of second serves that you can depend on to keep your opponent guessing. By changing your serves in a game, you may keep the opponents unsettled, helping you to win your serve more often. Try not to be the player who blasts her first serve, only making 10 percent of them, and follows up with a predictable weak second serve that your opponents will quickly figure out how to nail. Make more of your first serves and keep your second serves challenging.

Slowing Down Time

Strive to be centered when your opponent hits her shot and stay focused on the ball throughout your response.

Writing this piece during the global response to the coronavirus pandemic, it seemed rather poetic to address the topic of slowing down. The pace of life took on a new tempo as I stayed home from work and distanced myself from colleagues, friends, extended family, and neighbors.

For me, the stay-at-home order created a time with fewer daily demands. It was a gift, enabling me to catch up on projects that had simmered on the back burner for months. Almost overnight, I found myself with ample time to fit in most of the tasks I needed to accomplish. In some ways, it reminded me of my favorite type of moment when I'm playing tennis.

I call this *tennis nirvana*, a moment of perfect happiness on the court. This is, of course, a state of mind, and it's the experience I desire the most each time I'm playing. When everything fits into place, and my actions are in sync with the game, it strangely feels like time slows down.

When I am fully in the moment, my awareness sharpens and everything seems to flow with ease. My eyes are on the ball as it approaches my racquet, makes contact with my strings, and rebounds to the opponent's end of the court while I recover for the next shot. It feels like I'm straddling real time and slow-motion time, and that there's ample time for everything to happen as I execute my shot.

For the microseconds this all takes place, the world is just me and the ball. My senses feel heightened while my body remains calm and controlled. My reactions happen more quickly, more easily, and without thoughts interfering. I feel I have bent or stretched time, squeezing more into the moment than I can do in my normal state. My performance is at its best.

The good news is that you, too, have the power to achieve this state of mind. But, first, you have to be in the right place at the right time with the right stance and mindset. This means that, as your opponent hits the ball, your mind is clear, and you're in the ready position while making a gentle hop—the *split step*—on the balls of both feet. This is the centering moment of the point. (For more about the split step, see my discussion in Court Thought, "Banana Split Step.")

If you're fully present in the centering moment, the receiving phase will come more easily. You'll push off from your split step and turn to receive a forehand or backhand, moving to (or sometimes away from) the ball, making micro-adjustments with your feet to optimize your setup for the shot. As you're setting up your body to hit the ball, you're simultaneously deciding on your target while keeping your head steady and eyes focused on the ball.

Next you'll move into the sending phase. As you watch the ball impact your strings, you may experience a *slow-motion* sensation. Enjoy those few microseconds, but recover quickly to the nearest home to center yourself and be ready for the next shot from your opponent. You must not delay. Once positioned, feel light on your feet, hold your racquet in the ready position, focus on the ball, and open your mind to respond to all possibilities as the cycle begins again (Stormon, 2019).

I'm not suggesting that you can *think* of all the steps at any given time. Your thinking mind actually needs to be quiet so the body can do what it's trained to do. That's why we practice, drilling new skills—one at a time—until they become habits we can use without thinking. When we play, we rely on these habits so we can keep our minds clear and be free to react to the action on the court.

The time between shots isn't long, but when you remain disciplined in following these steps, the effect expands time. You will be more likely to fit everything in to execute a good shot, one after the other, after the other. The key is to reset yourself during the centering phase. If you can stay focused, there may be moments when it feels like time slows down.

So, be in the moment, whether it's on the tennis court or elsewhere in your life. The rewards will be greater when you keep your focus undivided. Essentially, it's all about experiencing each moment to its fullest.

Take a Stand

Stand your ground to occupy positions on the court that give you an offensive advantage or discourage your opponents from using a winning shot.

Tactics used in doubles tennis always account for the players' locations on the court. Where you stand when the ball is in the opponents' end of the court will have an impact on both your offensive and defensive potential. Whether it's the beginning of the point, or anytime during the point, your strength as a team depends on optimizing your positioning at your end of the court.

Positioning can be used to discourage your opponent from using a particular shot such as a lob or precision down-the-line forehand. It can also put a player in the most advantageous spot to place a winner. Therefore, it's important to learn how to use your position effectively to stand your ground against your opponent.

Most points begin in a typical starting formation with server and receiver in the back of the court. Server's partner is close to the net with receiver's partner on the service line.

Questions may arise about alternative starting formations and potential restrictions about where players are allowed to stand at the start of a point. In my experience, these questions have come up a couple of times in USTA matches where players were less familiar with the unconventional starting formations we were using.

Only the server is restricted to a defined location on the court: behind the baseline, between the center mark and the doubles sideline, on the deuce or the ad side of the court, depending on the point. The receiver, the receiver's partner, and the server's partner may stand almost anywhere on the their respective sides of the net which allows for a great deal of variety for where players may stand as the point begins.

For example, if server's partner is poaching well off the service return, receiver's partner may start on the baseline instead of the service line, thereby discouraging the server's partner from making the winning shot in the gap between the two partners. Alternatively, server's partner can start the point on the baseline beside her partner.

This was a tactic we employed as the serving team when the receiver kept lobbing my partner successfully. To prevent the opponent from sending a lob over her again, my partner joined me at the baseline to start the point. Our choice was effective, and we ended up winning the game.

We also could have chosen for my partner to stand farther back in the service box to discourage the opponent from lobbing. By standing nearer the service line, she would be in a better position to cover the lob.

Another time, playing at a sectional tournament, my opponent called over an umpire when she believed our starting formation was illegal. We were actually using Australian formation, whereby the server's partner starts close to the net, on the same side of the court as the server.

In fact, this is absolutely legal and can set up good poaching opportunities for the server's partner. It also discourages the receiver from hitting crosscourt.

Obviously, there are optimal and suboptimal locations for players
when changing from standard starting formations. Don't choose ι
in your defense or that throw off the server, leading to a double fauḷ.

Changing the starting positions can be good defense. It's also impoɪ
ground to make your offense more effective. In particular, you must pḷ
distance from the net as the net player, once the point is under way, to maintạ
advantage.

As a coach, I often observe that players don't stand close enough to the net. A   ɹ's
partner, they should begin the point in the middle of the service box. As receiver's partner,
they should move up from their starting location at the service line to the middle of the
service box at the appropriate time during the point. By hanging back at the service line,
they are automatically putting themselves on defense and giving up their ability to attack.

As the net player, stand in the middle of the service box and watch the ball when it is in front
of you. When the ball is behind, fade back a few steps towards the T (where the service line
meets the center line), watching the other net player and getting ready to defend if she hits
the ball. As soon as the ball passes her, you need to quickly move back to your home in the
middle of the service box and be ready to strike. (For more information about moving up
and back in the service box, see my discussion in Court Thought, "No Place Like Home.")

Many players feel uncomfortable playing close to the net and shy away from the correct
position in the service box.

- They may incorrectly start too far back as server's partner and never move up to
  where they can play offensive tennis.

- They may correctly start at the service line as receiver's partner but never move
  up to the offensive zone once the ball is past the other net player.

- They may stand at the correct location early in the point but slowly retreat as the
  point goes on.

As a result, they pass up many opportunities to attack the ball and score points. If they try
to attack the ball from too far back in the service box, most of their shots will end up in
the net.

...maintaining the correct distance from the net and being aggressive at the appropriate times. In tandem, you should develop confidence in your volleying skills as well as learn to discern when it's appropriate to take a shot as the net player or to leave a shot for your partner. Experience is the only way to develop a feel for effective net play.

In the beginning, you may feel uncomfortable standing close to the net. As you develop your skills, you will probably make mistakes trying for balls that should be left for your partner. You may feel overly excited and tense because the pace of play at the net is quicker than it is at the baseline, causing you to hit many balls into the net. But all of this is a part of normal development and should be accepted as part of the journey. Don't let these mistakes discourage you from trying.

So, learn where to be to optimize court coverage and find the confidence to stand your ground. Use tactically smart court positioning throughout the point to play better offense and defense as a doubles team. This, in combination with improved consistency, will take your game to the next level.

> To highlight a rule that is little known, it *is* legal for the receiver or receiver's partner to stand in the service box when receiving serve. However, they should be aware that if the serve hits them before it bounces, the point will go to their opponent.

Taking Sides

In doubles tennis, play on the same side of the court (ad side or deuce side) for an entire set when you're the receiving team.

In doubles tennis, teams take turns serving and receiving games. Players new to doubles are frequently confused about where they should stand to start the point.

I remember learning this was like learning the steps of a dance. It was easier to remember what to do as the serving team, where the server alternates sides to begin each new point. Her partner switches sides with her, from the ad- (left) side to the deuce- (right) side, and back again until the game is over.

The harder part of the dance to remember was when I was on the receiving team. Instead of switching sides with your partner, receiving team partners must stay on the same side of the court—one on the ad side, one on the deuce side—and take turns starting the point from the baseline or the net. They stay on their chosen sides to start each point, and when they are positioned at the baseline, they are the player who receives the serve.

At the beginning of a set, the receivers choose their designated sides and start each point of the game from there. They play on their chosen sides for an entire set as receivers. It's not until the set is over that they have the option to play as receivers on the other side, again for the entire set. This rule also applies between the second set and a third-set tiebreak.

Your position may change to the other side during the middle of a point if you switch sides with your partner to cover a lob. But when the next point begins, receiving team players must resume their designated sides of the court.

My coach provides guidelines in her book for choosing which side to play as receiving-team partners, based on players' attributes—mental, physical, and technical (Stormon, 2019). Choosing sides is something you should ideally work out before the match begins. It's important, perhaps even crucial, to the outcome of the match.

Think about it; you'll actually be playing on your side for approximately three-quarters of all the points, (half of the time when on the serving team and the entire time when on the receiving team), so it's important that you are very comfortable and effective playing on your chosen side.

As you'd expect, there are different considerations for right-handed versus left-handed players. Does your partner have the same dominant hand as you, or does she have the opposite? In the case of a right-handed and left-handed partnership, your choice of sides may have an effect on your court coverage, as you'll either have both forehands in the middle or both on the outside.

If you've lost the first set, occasionally it's a good tactical choice to change sides when you start the new set. This can throw off your opponents as they have to get used to the different arrangement, and they may find their offense is less effective against your team when you've done this.

Changing sides also gives your team the opportunity to use different tactics to defend or to score and win more points depending upon the strengths and specialty shots of each player. Even though this tactic can be effective, consider the decision carefully because you won't be able to change back in the middle of the set if it doesn't work out in your favor.

As a beginner, it's probably best to learn to play and become comfortable receiving from both sides. This means that in some sets or matches you'll play on the deuce side, and in others you'll play on the ad. Over time, you may discover that you have a preference for playing one side more than the other, in which case you can specialize as an ad-side or deuce-side player.

As a specialist on a particular side of the court, you're encouraged to develop one or two specialty shots that are effective for that side. For example, on the deuce side, a down-the-line shot off a wide ball can be very effective. Also, developing consistency with your lob over the opposing net player is a good play to learn as it puts the other team on defense.

On the ad side, if you're right-handed, using your forehand to pass the net player down the alley is an easy shot to learn and can be quite effective. If you're left-handed, developing the down-the-alley forehand passing shot will pay dividends. Another good shot to rely on from the ad side is a deep crosscourt shot to the (right-handed) opponent's backhand.

My partner and I played one USTA season as deuce- and ad-side specialists. During the following few months of the off-season, we used the opportunity to try out playing on the other side to gain proficiency. Becoming a specialist on one side of the court can give you and your partner advantages. However, having the versatility to play both sides, even if you primarily play one side, gives you more tactical opportunities.

Have fun trying out both sides, identifying and developing your strengths. If you don't play with the same doubles partner all of the time, you may discover you play well on one side of the court with a particular partner, but with a different partner, you may complement each other if you play the other side. As you make these discoveries, the information you gain will help you to solidify doubles partnerships with one or two regular partners, thereby creating competitive doubles teams.

Please note these two points of clarification: First, when you are warming up with your opponents before a match, you don't have to warm up on the side on which you plan to receive once the game begins. Second, your choice of receiving sides has nothing to do with which partner will serve first, regardless of who receives on the deuce side.

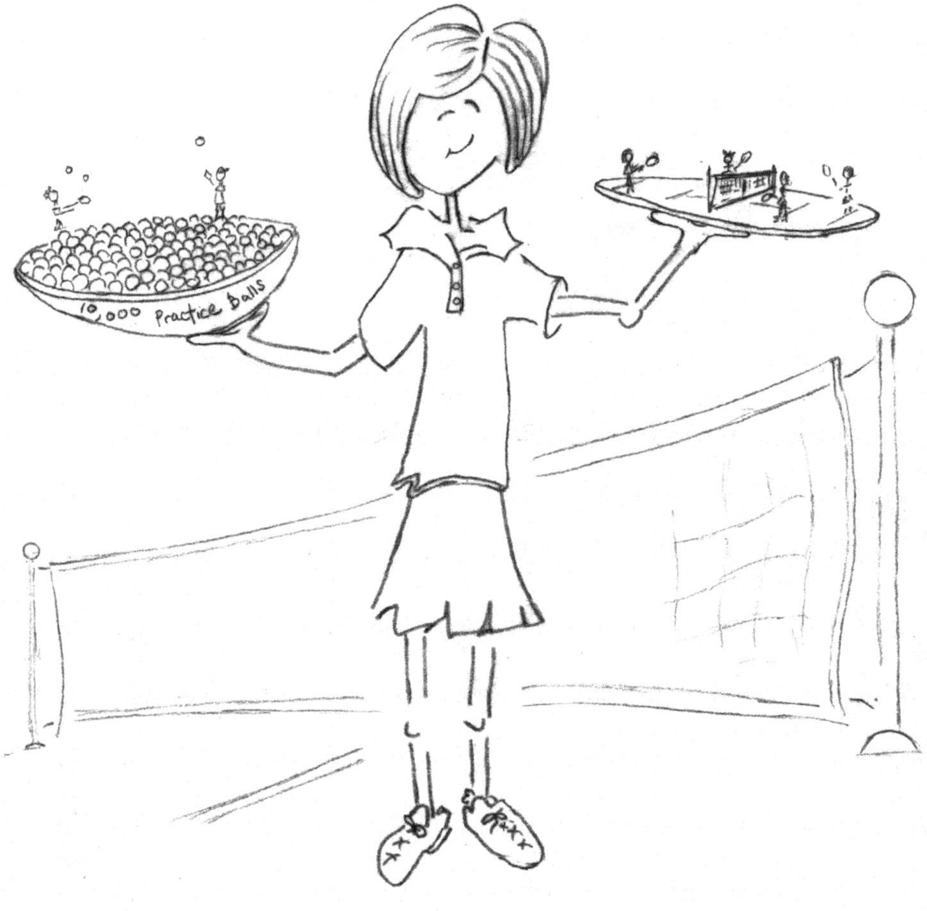
10,000 Practice Balls

Tennis Diet

If you're making changes to your game, a balanced tennis diet consists of a minimum of two practice sessions for every one time you play.

Practice makes perfect...or so the saying goes. In reality, there really is no *perfect* because we can always improve, no matter how good we are. For tennis players, this holds true because the game is a complex mixture of techniques and tactics, creating challenges with no limits.

We improve through practice, but practice alone will not advance your tennis game. Neither will spending all your time on the court in match play.

You need to participate in a mixture of practice and play in order to optimize your rate of improvement. The question is, what is a good mixture of these to help you reach your tennis goals?

First, determine what your goals are. Ask yourself the following questions:

- Are you playing simply for the fun of it and just want to play? If yes, then read no further. You probably won't advance very far or very fast if you don't mix in practice, but if this doesn't impede your enjoyment on the tennis court, then the choice to not practice will work for you.

- Are you content with the level you've reached in your tennis game and just want to maintain it? If yes, then you probably want to practice once in a while to maintain your skills but spend most of the time on the court in match play.

- Are you seeking to change your game, improving the skills you have and/or learning new ones? If your answer is yes, then according to Ian Westermann of Essential Tennis, you should be practicing twice for every time you play in a match (Westermann, 2018).

I'm still in the phase of my tennis journey seeking continuous improvement. When the USTA season ended for me last year, I was playing two matches per week. In order to make changes to my game in the off-season, I've followed Ian's advice and have added in a mixture of four to five lessons or drills per week. I believe this tennis diet works, as is evidenced by the steady improvement I've made to my game across the board: groundstrokes, volleys, lobs, and serves, as well as my tactical court awareness and coverage.

Ian explains that this formula works for a couple of reasons. First, lots of repetitions are required for our brains to learn new skills and turn them into habits. I might add that repetition is needed for improvement of both technical and tactical skills. Practice provides the opportunity for many more repetitions of a chosen skill than you would randomly get to do in a game. Some of us may even require hitting as many as 10,000 balls to learn a new skill, especially if it involves a complex technical change.

If, for example, you're working on your backhand groundstroke and you only played matches, it would take a long time to achieve a sufficient number of repetitions to master the stroke. Or, if you're working on approaching the net followed by your first volley, you may only get to attempt this one, two, or three times in a doubles game, and then only when you're starting from the baseline as server or receiver. However, if you practice this skill, you can repeat this combination of approach and volley multiple times in a row.

Second, when you play in a match, you don't have time to think about or analyze how to execute a shot. Since your focus is primarily on your opponents and the ball, you have to let your body react to the situation on the court. This usually means you automatically revert to the habits most ingrained in you. To convert a new skill into a habit, you must practice the new skill more times than you use the old one. This means you need to practice a new skill at least twice for every time you play a game. If you only practice once for each time you play, then you will be unlearning the new habit as many times as you attempt learning it.

Therefore, tennis practice, as opposed to match play, is essential if you want to improve your game. This will allow you to

- focus on one skill at a time,
- experiment with the parameters of a skill,
- take risks as you push your limits without the penalty of losing a game, and
- execute a meaningful number of repetitions of the skill you are trying to master.

Like our edible diet, a tennis diet is richer if you incorporate a mixture of activities, both on and off the court. On the court, your practice diet can be comprised of a variety of physical activities including these:

- drills with a coach for hitting lots of live balls and receiving feedback on technique
- lessons with a coach to learn both technique and tactics
- hitting with a practice partner for lots of repetitions in a live ball situation
- ball machine practice to provide repetitions for practicing a particular stroke

Off the court, video can be a powerful tool that you can use to improve your skills. You can watch videos that teach a particular skill; there are lots of tennis videos on the internet. Or you can record your practice session and learn from watching the videos of you in action. The use of video can give you feedback if you don't have a coach watching you. Plus, you may think you are executing a shot in a particular way, but video may reveal evidence contrary to your assumptions. (See my discussion in Court Thought, "Listen to Your Body" for more ideas about off-court practice.)

Above all, clarify your goals. If you're seeking to improve your game, identify the first thing you think will have the biggest impact on your game and focus on it during your practices. Then, practice more than you play and work hard to learn or improve one skill at a time. Once you've achieved consistency with one skill, move on to the next focus point on your list. You may find that you reach a level where you are content to remain, or you may be like me, where you're hungry to learn the next thing to improve your game. As long as you seek to make changes, ensure your progress by sticking to a prescribed and well-rounded tennis diet.

Tennis Technician

*Investing time and effort to master proper technique early in your tennis
journey will pay dividends down the road.*

I find great satisfaction working on tennis technique. The mechanics fascinate me, and I enjoy the process of learning and acquiring skills. It's intriguing to experiment with various ways of executing a shot and figuring out how to get the best results.

As a research scientist by training, experimentation and a dogged approach to mastering technical challenges are in my nature. When I worked in vaccine research, rarely did I go from point A to point B in an experiment without having to systematically troubleshoot to get things to work. But once I overcame a roadblock, the reward was sweet.

My tennis journey has been similarly rich with technical challenges. The scientist in me wants to execute strokes with precision. And, if I'm honest, a bit of vanity makes me want to look and feel the part of a professional. I get pleasure from performing with grace and good form.

I also feel a satisfying buzz when I observe that a well-executed stroke presents a challenge to my opponent. As a result, I spend lots of time working on technique.

When I was a beginning player, however, I was overwhelmed with the volume of new information I was taking onboard. My head felt full—too many variables to think about.

Assuming I could get away with it, I decided to simplify my number of court thoughts and abandoned one of the earlier fundamentals that we learn in tennis, the grip change. My solution was to use one grip for all strokes because it was one less thing to think about.

The problem with using one grip for all strokes was that my consistency stunk. Eventually, after more than a year, I realized I had to face the music and revisit this topic to learn to use the proper grip for each stroke. It was a bit of a setback in my training, but in the end, it was well worth it. In hindsight, it would have been much easier if I had stuck with learning to change grip in the first place.

The thing is, some players with poor—even hideous—technique can have very effective games. These are usually self-taught players who have learned to send back an extraordinary number of balls. These players are sometimes known as *pushers* or *hacks*. They can actually be infuriating to play against because their unconventional technique hinders you from getting into a rhythm.

A particular USTA doubles match comes to my mind when thinking about this type of player. My partner and I got the impression, from the warm-up and first two games of the match, that our opponents were just a bit beyond beginner level. They did not seem to know the steps of the standard 10-minute warm-up, and they looked odd when they hit the ball as they didn't use techniques my partner and I recognized.

We won the first two games fairly easily, at which point we concluded that we were the better team and would probably zip this up 6-0, 6-0. To our astonishment, our opponents pulled ahead and ended up winning the match, primarily because we had failed to respect their ability, despite their unconventional technique.

Especially in doubles, players like these, who possess unusual spins and can also send both short shots and effective lobs, will win a lot of matches. So what is the downside, you might ask? There are two main concerns: the inability to move beyond a certain level and the risk of injury.

Sometimes players simply don't know their technique is wrong. They've not had a coach advise them. For example, they may not have an effective volley, but they don't know why and may assume it will improve with time. Or they choose to hang back at the baseline where they are more confident and never play up at net.

Then there are players who know their technique isn't right but choose to ignore it. They may think that having unconventional technique won't matter as long as they're able to get the ball back over the net. Or perhaps they have played this way for years and don't have the patience or desire to put in the time and energy to change. These players justify their choice *to leave well enough alone* because they manage to get away with mediocre technique. They would rather just get on with the game.

But, in the long run, players with compromised technique will eventually plateau. They can't move beyond a certain skill level because they are missing some fundamental technical elements in their game. At this point, they either have to pause their journey to learn the skills they skipped, or they decide they're fine staying at the level they've reached.

Ignoring proper technique can result in poor ball control and put you on the defense more than the offense. If you don't learn to generate good topspin with your groundstrokes, use the correct grip when hitting volleys, or toss the ball high enough for your serve, you won't realize your potential.

If you favor your forehand over your backhand and set up to take most shots this way, your opponent may spot this early on and exploit it. She may target your backhand, hoping to widen the gap between you and your partner so that she or her partner can send the next shot between you and win the point. Therefore, take the time to improve your backhand and become confident using it.

A more serious consequence of playing with bad technique is the risk of injury such as tennis elbow or wrist inflammation. In order to continue playing tennis at all, these players must make changes, unlearning the bad habit and practicing the new one until it becomes ingrained. This takes extra time and effort in addition to the healing process that must happen first.

I believe that proper technique is worth learning because it is tied to playing well, improving, and staying healthy. If you're new to the game, be patient with yourself.

As you focus on one new technique at a time, don't abandon the others. Write them down in your court notebook so that you can work through them systematically as you make your journey. Trust that it is worth your initial investment to pursue good technique, not for the sake of perfection, but for the sustainable progress you will continue to make along the way.

Tiebreaks

If you play a tiebreak, stay calm, focused, and stick to your game. Don't take risks or try strategies you haven't practiced.

Some of the best tennis matches end up in tiebreaks to decide the winner of a set or the winner of the entire match. I suggest that when we reach a tiebreak, it's the best tennis because it often means players were well-matched, scores were close, and most likely, the points were interesting.

I've learned that tiebreaks are nothing to fear or dread. They follow a standard format. The best way to feel comfortable and prepared to play tiebreaks is to practice them during team practices or casual matches where you may have an extra 10 or 15 minutes of court time remaining after your game is over. If you have time, it's helpful to change ends as you would in a match so you get used to the rhythm.

This will help familiarize you with the mechanics of tiebreaks as well as teaching you the importance of staying focused. I've discovered that if you practice tiebreaks enough so that they feel routine, it will free you up in a match to focus on each point in the tiebreak and give you the chance to be more successful.

One of the main differences between a regular game and a tiebreak is that the server changes more frequently, so players do not have time to settle into a groove. Players need to be mindful from the beginning of each point to its conclusion, stick with play until the point is definitely over, and then reset quickly for the next point.

Sometimes when you think a ball is going out or going into the net, you disengage mentally before the point is actually over. It is particularly important during tiebreaks to be mentally sharp, even more so than during a regular game.

Aside from the intense focus and the mechanics of a tiebreak that dictate which side to serve from, the serve rotation, changing ends of court, and scorekeeping, the other important things to remember are to breathe, to share a smile with your partner, and to stick to your game. This will help you manage the pressure.

Beware of trying shots you haven't practiced or used in the match. This will create more mistakes and send you into a downward spiral of lost points which may justifiably worry you.

When the pressure is on, don't panic; let the other team make the mistakes. A tiebreak is the time to remain consistent, focused, capitalize on your strengths to stay in the match, one point at a time.

This is one of the reasons it is advisable to try different plays such as Australian serve formation early on in a match, to warm it up and to see if it's effective against the other team. Sprinkle them into your first set. Don't save them as surprise tactics at the end when the pressure is on and mistakes may cost you more dearly.

If you found that you scored points using a different tactic early in the match, then it may be sensible to use that tactic in the tiebreak, especially if you need to change things up. As Peter Scales advises in his book *Mental and Emotional Training for Tennis*, "Always change a losing game, never change a winning game." But don't go crazy and change a losing game with something you've rarely practiced.

Never give up in a tiebreak. There is always a chance to come back no matter how far behind you are. This happens surprisingly often, perhaps because nerves are usually high for all players, and momentum shifts can occur quite swiftly.

If you're down in the match, consistency will be your safest bet for coming back. Don't become unsettled, don't be rash in decision-making, and don't try risky plays or shots you are still learning. That means stick to what you know and sharpen your focus to execute that well.

Of course, you should adjust small things like serve placement if your serve to the opponent's forehand results in the opponent scoring on you. Likewise, your court position might be adjusted slightly to discourage a lob. But don't try to serve and volley in a tiebreak if you haven't been practicing this or using it in the match.

I like to make the other team play my game in a tiebreak while I keep focused on one ball at a time. Remember, the difference between winning or losing can be a matter of two points. Plus, if you feel confident when faced with a tiebreak, your confidence will help you succeed.

Tip for the Server

Master your ball toss with steady practice off and on the court to ensure a successful serve, and when serving in a game, only hit a good toss.

When I was learning to serve in tennis, I found the ball toss to be challenging, as do most beginners. Several times each week, I would go out in my garage, where the ceiling is very high, and practice my ball toss 100 times. It was an easy thing to do at home, and my diligence paid off when I practiced serving on the tennis court.

A good serve is ensured by a good ball toss. Therefore, if you toss the ball and it's a poor toss, don't hit it. Catch it and toss it again. Only hit the ball when you've executed a good toss. This, in itself, takes a little discipline, especially if you have to toss it two or three times.

What makes a good toss and how do you practice this? A good ball toss will fulfill a specific three-dimensional location with respect to your body. An optimal height, distance in front, and position to the side of you are the three spatial coordinates that must be achieved.

This discussion focuses on the coordinates for a good, standard ball toss. As you progress in your serving ability, there are times when you'll vary your toss for a specific effect such as putting spin on your serve.

A ball toss can be practiced both on and off the tennis court. Before you begin, be attentive to the proper setup. If you're off the court, let's say on your driveway, it's useful to place a marker on the ground to serve as a baseline for your orientation. Use a 2-foot strip of tape or anything that will lay flat. If you're practicing on the court, set up behind the baseline as though you're serving in a real game.

Stand sideways to the baseline or the marker with your front foot (left foot for right-handers, right foot for left-handers) at an angle with your toes turned out slightly. If you're on the court, your front foot will be pointed toward the right net post for right-handed players or at the left net post for left-handed players.

Place your back foot parallel to the baseline or marker so that it's about hip width from your front foot. Feel balanced with your weight evenly distributed.

Next, think about where you need to toss the ball. You'll be aiming for a specific three-dimensional location in relation to where you're standing.

For the first dimension, height, aim to toss the ball just a bit higher than your racquet can reach with your arm upwardly outstretched. It's very common for beginners to execute a short toss out of fear of losing control.

Tossing the ball high enough gives the server more time to swing the racquet, allows for the correct timing as the toss and swing are coordinated, and results in reaching up for the ball with the racquet, which together make a better serve. Note that when you're practicing your toss 100 times, you may need to begin with a lower toss as you hone the other two dimensions, then gradually increase your toss to the correct height.

Second, the distance you toss the ball in front of you should be about as far as your arm extends straight out from your body. When playing, if the ball goes too far forward, catch it and toss it again. If the toss comes back over your head, catch it and toss it again. You are allowed as many tosses as it takes for you to execute a toss worth hitting.

The third dimension determines where in front you should toss the ball, either to the left or to the right of your body. When you are facing the court, imagine a large clock face directly ahead. If you are a right-handed player, toss the ball to the 1 o'clock position of the clock face. If you are a left-handed player, your toss should be to 11 o'clock on the imaginary clock face.

Now that you've assumed the correct setup and know where to toss the ball, you're ready to practice the toss. First, hold your racquet in one hand and a ball in your other, resting it between the thumb and your index finger, with the middle finger supporting it from underneath.

When you're first learning, propel your arm upwards from its starting position beside your thigh, holding the ball as long as you can before releasing it. Eventually you'll probably start your service motion with the racquet and ball touching, then drop the tossing arm down to the hip before lifting it up again.

The movement comes from your shoulder, not the wrist or elbow. You'll want the ball to move straight up, without any spin, in the area that fulfills the three spatial coordinates described above. Leave the tossing arm up high for an extra moment after you release the ball. This helps with better balance and will encourage you to reach up for the ball as you hit it.

Don't be discouraged if it takes a great deal of practice to develop a consistent toss. Most of us are not used to tossing a ball with our non-dominant hand, so take the time to train this new movement.

As you become proficient with a stable and straight toss, you'll need to coordinate the racquet swing with the toss. As your skills improve, you will advance to starting with the ball and racquet pressed together at waist height, then separating them as you drop the tossing arm down to its starting position, simultaneously bringing the racquet back with your other hand.

If your serve needs work, practice your ball toss 100 times per day, on or off the court. With the correct setup and the three spatial coordinates for placing the ball, you can expect your diligent practice to lead to greater consistency in your serve. If you can master this one aspect of the serve, you will succeed with the rest of your serve much sooner and be more confident during a game when the pressure is on.

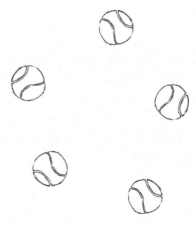

To Everything, Turn, Turn, Turn

For every shot, get turned.

It always amazes me when making a simple change results in a big impact on outcome. In this case, I'm talking about turning sideways before executing a stroke.

I was attending my regular lesson when my coach gave me the advice to get turned more before hitting my forehand. The funny thing is that I thought I was turned, but my shots lacked power. So I took her advice on board and turned even more as I set myself up for the shot. It felt exaggerated at first because I'd only been partially turning previously. Now I was fully turning.

The results of this simple adjustment to my stroke blew me away! My forehand groundstrokes sailed to the other end of the court with relative ease.

We're supposed to do this for every shot we make whether it is a volley, an overhead, a serve, or a groundstroke. The mechanics of the stroke demand that, at the very least, our upper bodies are sideways. This position allows our joints and muscles to perform with the most ergonomically optimal mechanics as we put our racquets in position to hit the ball.

Facing the net as we prepare to hit the ball is a common mistake. This is natural since we're facing the action in our centering moment. But as soon as we see the ball is going to travel to our backhand or forehand, we need to turn. Since this lesson, my court thought as receiver is *get turned*.

I have found this is a good reminder to set myself up to return a serve most effectively. On the return, decide whether you'll be hitting the ball on your forehand or backhand side and get turned first. Then run forward, back, or sideways if needed.

For volleys, we often have less time to react, but we need to make every effort to get turned, even if we haven't time to move our feet. We can at least rotate our upper bodies before we hit.

Overheads are commonly hit straight on, but this is just bad technique. If you execute that stroke as you're turned sideways, you will not only hit a better shot, your arm will suffer less abuse.

It's also important to remember that as you move back for some lobs, you need to turn first and move back sideways. This movement pattern may take some time to learn and will also require practice, but it is important. Moving straight back risks falling backwards and injuring yourself.

If you find you don't execute good directional control of the ball with your strokes, often sending the ball off the sides of the court or directly into the strike zone of your opponent, stop where you are when the point ends and assess your stance. You may find that you can turn your game around by focusing your attention on this basic technical aspect to all your strokes, simply by turning sideways to the court to set up for a better shot. This one improvement may help you direct your shots to the intended target with greater consistency and add power to your groundstrokes and overheads with greater ease.

Trust and Teamwork

*When playing doubles tennis, know your roles,
trust your partner, and work as a team.*

Growing up, I was never a fan of playing team sports. I wasn't confident in my athletic ability and disliked the idea of other players relying on me as a teammate. When I began playing tennis, that feeling carried over, and I felt more comfortable playing singles because I was only accountable to myself.

However, I soon discovered there were more opportunities to play doubles than singles. It also became evident that doubles was quite a different game to singles, and its many strategic aspects intrigued me. Ultimately, I grew to love the challenge of doubles tennis, and as I've pursued this journey, I've had to embrace the virtue of trust.

This does not require a huge leap of faith if you take the time to learn and practice the roles and responsibilities of each doubles team player. Once you understand what parts of the court you must cover, where your optimal targets are, and what balls to take or leave for your partner, your confidence will enable you to trust yourself and your doubles partner.

In doubles tennis, partners most commonly assume the one-up and one-back formation. This places one player behind the baseline on one side of the court (ad side or deuce side) and the other player closer to the net in the service box, on the other side of the court. They are referred to as the baseline player and the net player, respectively, and have different roles to fulfill in the partnership.

The primary role of the baseline player is setting up her partner to score. That means keeping the ball in play and sending challenging shots to the opponents in order to weaken their responses. Once the baseline player has pierced the opponents' armor, her partner may find an opportunity to score the point from her advantageous position close to the net.

This means the baseline player should send the ball crosscourt the majority of the time and will be hitting the ball more often than her partner until the moment arises when the net player can successfully intercept. Doing this requires patience from both partners.

The net player needs to wait for the right ball to effectively poach, and the baseline player needs to hit crosscourt the majority of the time without giving in to the temptation to end the point early. Consistently keeping the ball in play crosscourt may result in an opportunity for your partner at net, or it may result in the other baseline player making the first mistake.

Once in a while, the baseline player may see the alley open up and take the chance of sending a down-the-line shot to win the point. Or a baseline player with a powerful forehand or backhand groundstroke may hit directly at the net player. But these are riskier moves, and the winning payoff is more likely to happen if the partnership works like a team as described above.

Often, a baseline player will rush the point and change direction from crosscourt to down the line, either with a passing shot down the alley or with a lob over the other net player. I have noticed this on some occasions regardless of the type of ball the baseline player has received. Premature termination of the point may risk losing it because these are lower-percentage shots, especially off a difficult ball.

When you are sent a difficult ball, aim to keep it in play and wait for an offensive opportunity. Trust yourself. Know you can keep the ball in play and be confident you can outlast your opponent.

As the baseline player, trust your doubles partner and give her the chance to find the opportunity to win the point from the net. Set her up by sending crosscourt balls that challenge the opposing baseline player. Hit deep, with pace, or make the opponent move, putting her on the defense. This gives your net player partner a chance to capitalize on a weak response and win the point. It's classic doubles play to achieve this.

When the baseline player has the patience to keep the ball in play, points last longer, thereby becoming more interesting and more fun. I love it when I'm playing with a partner who sets me up at net. It sends me a strong message that my partner trusts my ability to strike when the opportunity presents itself and gives me the chance to feel the exhilaration of ending the point with a poach.

As the net player, trust your doubles partner to keep the ball in play and don't poach balls that are difficult to score on. Wait for the right ball, keeping your eyes either on the ball when it's in front of you or on the other net player when the ball is behind you.

Don't look back at your partner unless she is receiving a high or deep ball and may not be able to call the line as she prepares to set up for the shot. In these instances, the net player can briefly glance back to make the line call on the baseline if needed.

Also trust your baseline partner to switch sides if you have to move across the court to reach a short wide ball. She will see what you are doing since you are in front of her. Likewise, if you are lobbed, trust your baseline partner to communicate, "Got it, switch," as she changes sides of the court to cover the lob and switch back quickly to the opposite service line.

Trust your skills from all of the practice you've invested in your game and trust the system. Learn to play high-percentage tennis: where to recover on the court; what the best options are for shot choice in various game situations; where are the most effective targets to aim for relative to your position, your partner's position, and your opponents' positions. If you practice them until they become habits, they will manifest as your primary responses without you having to think.

Remember, if you are the baseline player, crosscourt, crosscourt, crosscourt! And if you are the net player, be patient. Don't risk hitting a ball that might have been easier for your partner to return. Trust your partner to set you up. Working together as a unit and supporting each other frees you both to play your best tennis. With practice, you may experience moments on the court where you and your partner are in sync and harmony.

Doubles tennis is not four individual players, each trying to win the point. It is all about teamwork, trusting your partner, knowing your role, and sharing responsibility. Like me, you may discover new delight in doubles tennis when you can build your self-confidence and develop the courage to play with a partner. Together, you win and lose points. Your successes should be attributed to your team, because as the old saying goes, "there is no *I* in teamwork."

Under Pressure

Learn how to play under pressure
as well as how to put pressure on your opponents.

When I was a fairly new player and struggling with how to deal with pressure in a match, my coach shared a quote from tennis great Billie Jean King: "Pressure is a privilege." How we handle that pressure, she explained, can make all the difference in how we play. Like most players, King experienced pressure, but she learned how to manage it and go on to win 39 Grand Slam titles. Do we expect King and other Grand Slam winners to be the only ones who can master pressure in a match? Or can we, as recreational players, learn to embrace this intense and often uncomfortable feeling so that it doesn't derail our performance?

Fortunately, you can learn to manage this mental gremlin, minimize the distractions created by high-stress situations, and focus on the elements that will enhance your performance. You can also learn how to put pressure on your opponent to win more points.

There are many causes to feeling under pressure on the tennis court:
- playing doubles and not wanting to let your partner down
- playing against an opponent you know to be a higher-level player
- playing against a team you're expected to beat

- playing against strangers
- being reminded by your doubles partner that you are facing match point
- playing with a new doubles partner and trying to find your rhythm
- playing on a team and knowing your match will determine the overall win or loss outcome for the team

For example, I was recently asked to sub for a group I'd never played with before. It was a last-minute thing as they were on the court waiting for their fourth player who had apparently forgotten about their match, and I was practicing serves on the next court over. I was pleased to be asked but felt nervous because I knew this group had many more years of playing experience than me.

All things considered, it was a great opportunity to play with better players, and it was kind of them to invite me, so I accepted. Almost immediately, my heart rate increased and my breathing became shallow. There was no warm-up since they'd already been there a while, and my first few shots were into the net or out, which made me feel more self-conscious. It was more stressful than fun, and I began to regret my decision to join them.

My initial solution was to focus with intensity and determination, but this didn't seem to help. My game felt like a disaster, and I wanted to tell them, "This isn't how I normally play!"

When I had time to check in with myself on the changeover, I realized the tension had ramped up and my body was very tight. As we took our places for the start of the next game, I knew I needed to be more relaxed to free myself up. I took a deep breath and slowly exhaled, reminding myself of the joy tennis gives me. I smiled. Things began to improve.

I worked hard the rest of the match to maintain a better state of mind. I took a deep breath when my opponent hit the ball, and I told myself I COULD do this. I also reminded myself why I was there—my love of tennis—and welcomed the challenge instead of fearing it.

In the end, my consistency was back on track, I hit enough winners, and I felt that I gave my opponents a reasonable challenge so that everyone had a good time. But, ironically, it was hard work to stay relaxed and fulfill my part. With practice, I have found this has become easier.

I recommend you play with people you don't know or haven't played with before. If you can do this on a regular basis, you'll learn to manage your inner stress, read your opponents, and respond with tactics that are effective without becoming unsettled in your game. I've made it a point to play once a week at a different tennis club where I don't know the players. I've had a good time experimenting with it as well as meeting lots of new people, and it has made playing with strangers easier.

Specifically, try these suggestions when feeling under pressure during play:

- Breathe and relax.
- Imagine the other player is someone you know.
- Stay focused on the ball and opponents instead of focusing on the score.
- Stick to what you know and do well, and don't be pushed into using risky moves you haven't practiced enough.
- Above all, believe in yourself.

The flip side of this coin is dishing out pressure to your opponents. As a developing player, look for opportunities to be offensive in your play or to make moves to weaken the opponents' offense.

- Moving closer to the net can be intimidating and distracting to the opponent. I tried this recently, and it forced my opponent to make riskier shots in order to avoid me. We won several points from these forced errors even though I never put my racquet on the ball.

- If you face a player who continuously lobs you, stand farther back in the court to take this advantage away from her.

- If you're faced with a returner who keeps sending the ball down the line, serve or hit to that player's weaker side so she cannot execute this shot as easily.

- Talk between points. This may give the perception that you are continuously strategizing when, in fact, you may just be supporting your doubles partner with words of encouragement. But the opponents do not know what is being said, and this can be a distraction to them.

Look for opportunities to apply pressure to your opponents and practice plays with your partner so you have some plans you can fall back on. Troubleshooting when you're down in a match can lead to some very successful outcomes as well as an empowering feeling that you and your partner aren't just the opponents' victims.

Embracing the challenge of pressure on the tennis court instead of fearing it will help you grow as a player. If you can learn from your experience, then even when you lose a match, you will come out stronger the next time you face this element on the court. But most of all, if you learn how to manage pressure, you will have a better time playing because you won't be uptight and nervous.

Warm Up Before the Warm-up

*Warming up your body and focusing your mind before you
go on the court is better for you, both physically and mentally,
and increases your chances of winning.*

I was trained to follow a standard 10-minute warm-up that includes mini-tennis, ground-strokes, volleys, overheads and serves before a tennis match begins. Ten minutes is a minimal time to warm up our bodies and engage our minds. If you find you don't perform well until the third or fourth game of a set, try warming up additional time before going onto the court.

Even if you are a player who performs well right from the beginning of a match, it is advisable to incorporate an adequate warm-up to avoid injuries when you play. There are many warm-up options, both with and without a tennis ball.

If you play tennis at a facility with a cardio room, hop on a treadmill for 10 minutes to warm up your muscles and get your blood flowing before walking onto the tennis court. If you are playing at an outdoor court, run a few laps around the court when you first go out, perhaps alternating with various footwork to keep it interesting and challenging.

If you're alone, or you and your partner are the only ones there, self-feed three balls to warm up crosscourt groundstrokes, then chase after the balls to pick them up and repeat until you've hit from all four corners of the court. This will get your blood pumping, your body warmed up, and prime your hand-eye coordination for your match play. Plus, it is fun and doesn't feel like a chore.

If others are on the court and you don't have the freedom to do the self-feeding warm-up, ball tosses and ghost swings are also good ways to switch on the tennis app in your brain to engage hand-eye coordination and the body movements we use in tennis. Spending as little as five minutes doing this before going out onto the court will make a difference in your readiness to play.

If your tennis facility has a wall you can hit against, use that as a warm-up exercise. Alternatively, you can hit against your garage door for 15 minutes before you leave home. Using foam balls or low-compression balls, such as orange balls, works well for this exercise as they don't rebound as far, plus they're less likely to damage your garage or outdoor light fixtures.

Watching live tennis, a tennis video, or closing your eyes and visualizing yourself swinging the racquet is another effective tool. Even go as far as moving your body and feeling the shot as you imagine executing a forehand or backhand groundstroke. I often *think* tennis when I am driving to the court, preparing my mental readiness.

Once last summer, I played one of my best games of tennis after watching my coach play in a match right before I went out onto the court. I believe it was because my brain had been primed.

All these options work well to warm up your body and prepare your mind before you step on the court for practice or routine play. However, if you are playing in an important tennis match, the ideal preparation is to warm up your body and then run through a 30- to 45-minute pre-match routine within an hour or two before arriving at the court for your match (Stormon, 2019). This will sharpen you both mentally and physically and also help to calm the nervousness that most players feel before a big match.

Warming up before the warm-up can help prevent injuries as well as enhance your preparedness to play. Set aside the extra time. It's a small investment for the return you'll get back. Practice this regime before match play for a couple of weeks and notice how you've elevated your game.

What's Love Got to Do with It?

*Be clear about how to score, what the score is,
and when you must play a tiebreak.*

As you may know, in unofficiated tennis matches, it's the server's job to call out the score at the start of each game and at the beginning of each point. Although this job is delegated to the server of that game, for practical reasons, all players on the court should be keeping score in their heads.

This is useful when distractions cause the server to make a mistake or lose track of the score. If other players are paying attention, they can help re-establish the score when help is needed.

Scoring involves points, games, sets, matches, and tiebreaks. A series of points make games, games make sets, and sets make matches. Winning is achieved by most points in a game, most games in a set, most sets in a match.

There are conventions to follow such as the rule of winning by two points in certain circumstances. And scoring is a bit odd because the first and second points in the sequence are worth 15 each, but the third number in the scoring sequence only increases by 10.

Then, once the score is tied at 40 all, you must win by two points, but each of those points has no actual numerical value. Sounds confusing, perhaps, but scoring in tennis is pretty straightforward, once you become familiar with it.

Games start out 0-0. In tennis, we say *love-love*, or a favorite of some is *love all around*. So, what's *love* got to do with it? *Love* is another word for "0." It comes from French, *l'oeuf* which means *the egg* because a zero looks like an egg. The word was Anglicized to *love* because of its similar sound.

The score progresses through the numbers 15, 30, 40, game. (Why 40, not 45?—see below). If it is tied at 40-40, a score also known as *deuce*, then the player must win by two points.

The score progresses from deuce to advantage-in or advantage-out meaning the server has either won or lost the next point respectively. The term advantage-in refers to the fact that if the server wins the next point, she has the advantage.

However, the word advantage is usually shortened to *ad* in informal matches. If the score is ad-out and the server wins the next point, the score goes back to deuce. Likewise, if the score is ad-in and the server loses the next point, the score goes back to deuce. If the score is deuce, and the same player (or team) wins the next two points in a row, then the game is over and that side wins.

Here is an example:

- The server wins the first point, so the score is 15-love. The server always announces her score first.

- The next point is won by the opponent, so the score is 15 all.

- The opponent wins the third point, so the score becomes 15-30.

- Then the opponent wins the fourth point, changing the score to 15-40. If the opponent were to win the next point, the game would be over, and the opponent would win the game.

- But at this point, the server digs deep and wins the next two points to stay in the game, so the score changes to 30-40 and then 40-40 (deuce). Now either side must win by two points.

- The opponent wins the next point, so the server announces the score as ad-out.

- The next point is won by the server, and the score goes back to deuce.

- Next, the server wins another point, and the score becomes ad-in.

- Finally, the server wins the next point, and the game is now over because the server won the last two points in a row.

The game score is now 1-0, but the opponent becomes the server for the next game, so she starts the game by announcing the game score 0-1.

The series of games continues until one player or team wins a set of six, sometimes seven, games. This can be 6-0, 6-1, 6-2, 6-3, or 6-4.

Now, remember the win-by-two rule, which applies to the number of games in a set as well. So, if the game score reaches 5-5, a team must win by two games so the score must reach 7-5. A score of 6-5 is not an endpoint.

To recap, a set can end 6-0, 6-1, 6-2, 6-3, 6-4, or 7-5.

However, if the score progresses 5-5, 6-5, then 6-6 (instead of 7-5), the winner is determined by continuing on to play a *set tiebreak*.

A seven-point set tiebreak is played once the score reaches 6-6. The winner is the first to seven points or beyond if required. Remember the win-by-two rule; she must win by at least two points (7-5, 8-6, 9-7). At the end of a tie break, the game score is recorded as 7-6 because the set tiebreak essentially counts as one game.

For recreational matches, the winner of the match is usually determined by winning best of three sets. If both teams win one set each, then rather than playing a regular third set, the winner of the third set is often determined by a 10-point *match tiebreak*. That means that the first team to win 10 points wins the third set and the match.

The win-by-two rule applies here as well, so if the score reaches 10-9, the match is not over yet. The winning team must win by two points: 10-8, 11-9, 12-10, and so on.

It is advised that set and match tiebreaks be practiced occasionally so that players are comfortable and familiar with them when they occur. USTA League uses the Coman Tiebreak System.

Sometimes no-ad scoring is used to accelerate matches in situations like social round-robins where players are trying to get through a maximum number of games in a fixed amount of time before the round ends when you change partners and opponents. High school and college tennis also use no-ad scoring, as do many professional doubles matches. No-ad scoring means that when the score reaches deuce, the next point determines the winner. Players don't have to win by two points. (For more information about no-ad scoring, see my discussion in Court Thought, "Eenie, Meenie, Minie, Moe.")

One final convention worth mentioning is the rule that governs changing ends of the court with your opponent and flipping the score card. This is particularly important when playing outdoors to give each opponent the same advantages of wind and sun by playing equal numbers of times on each end of the court. After each odd game (1,3,5…), players switch ends of the court.

It is at this time only that the score cards should be flipped. This was clearly explained to us last summer at a USTA Sectionals match by the court official. He said that players must only flip the score cards on the changeover (when changing ends), because some players have been known to flip cards after even games (when players don't change ends) as a delay tactic to throw off the rhythm of the server. Likewise, the score cards should not be used to keep track of the points in a tiebreak.

Therefore, when you are playing a friendly match, practice this convention of only flipping the card when players change ends. It will also be good practice to remember the game scores every two games. It's another reason all players on the court should keep track of the scores, in case mistakes are made when flipping the cards after more than one game has been played.

Like all things, scoring tennis takes practice as does learning the mechanics of a tiebreak. The more you do it, the easier it will become and the more comfortable you'll feel on the court.

Practice keeping score, not only when you're serving, but when you're the server's partner or the receiving team. Pay close attention to the score when you're playing a tiebreak, especially because the score cards are not used at this time, and we must rely on memory.

When it's your turn to serve, be sure to announce the score loudly enough so that all players on the court can hear what you've said. That way, mistakes can be corrected immediately. Developing good scorekeeping skills enhances the etiquette on the court and keeps disputes at a minimum. And above all, remember what *love's* got to do with it!

Why 40, not 45? Historically, tennis scoring dates back to medieval times in France. Apparently, a clock face was used as the device to keep score. For every point, the clock hand was advanced a quarter of an hour, thus 0, 15, 30, 45, and 60 were the points. However, because of the win-by-two rule, 45 was reduced to 40 so that the winning point could still be 60, the last minute on a clock face before the next revolution of 0-60. After 30, each successive point was plus 10, so the scoring progressed 0, 15, 30, 40, 50, ending with 60.

You Be the Judge

Learn to judge different types of ball bounces and where to move in order to
reach them and optimize your return.

When I started learning to play tennis, like many other beginners, one of the biggest errors I made when executing groundstrokes was moving too close to where the ball bounced right before I would strike it. Running into the ball, as my coach called it, caused me to make impact when the ball was much too high in its descent after it bounced, often chest to shoulder high.

This not only made me feel jammed up, but I was not able to execute a good stroke because my reaction to hitting a high ball caused my swing path to move from high (where the ball was) to low. Hitting down on the ball, I often dumped it into the net.

The next time you're out on the tennis court, send a groundstroke to the other end of the court and watch it bounce twice. The path it travels will be two arcs. Note that after you hit the ball, it rises to a peak, then descends until it bounces and completes the first arc.

The bounce pops the ball up again where it rises to a second peak and descends to complete the second arc. During the time the ball travels the path of this second arc, it rises, peaks, descends. Likewise, you can hit it as it rises, when it peaks, or as it descends. All have their own merit.

However, in the beginning, you must learn to position yourself to strike the ball on the way down. It's during the descent, after it has bounced once, that it's easiest to hit. As you become more advanced, you will learn to hit it on the way up (called *on the rise*) and at the peak.

We know from training that to generate a good topspin forehand stroke, the swing path must go from low to high with our racquets hitting the back side of the ball in the process. If the ball is shoulder high at impact, it is quite difficult to continue to swing the racquet even higher after impact in order to follow through using the low to high swing path.

The goal is to hit the ball when it has descended to a height above the ground that is somewhere between your waist and hips. This lower ball position invites you to drop your racquet on the take back, swing low to high on impact, and finish your swing with a higher follow-through.

Executing this properly will develop good ball control and consistency in your game. This is why it's important to develop a sense of predicting where the ball will be after it bounces.

Judging the ball well requires experience through practice, receiving a variety of balls hit hard, soft, short, deep, high, and low to the net. Pay attention to the type of ball you're receiving (height, speed, direction), to where the ball bounces, and to where it enters your hitting zone.

You can do this by observing where the ball bounces the first time, then instead of hitting it, let it continue to travel and bounce a second time. I remember my coach telling us that to be in the right position to hit the ball on its descent after the first bounce, you actually have to be standing where it would bounce the second time.

When you're rallying with your practice partner, pay attention to where you must be positioned relative to the ball bouncing in front of, at, or behind the service line in order to hit it well. As a starting point for judging where to be in relation to the incoming ball, be ready to receive the ball at your baseline home (which is just behind the baseline), and

- when the ball bounces between the net and the service line, you will probably have to move into the court a step or two (in the transition zone aka no man's land) to hit the ball after it descends to waist height;

- when the ball bounces close to or on the service line, you may not have to move forward or backward at all to hit the ball at the correct height;

- when the ball bounces between the service line and the baseline, you should anticipate moving back several steps behind the baseline so you are well-positioned to hit the ball when it has descended to waist height. Being far enough back also allows you to judge whether or not a ball will bounce out of the court, in which case you should not hit it.

This information will help you to adjust your position on the court in the receiving phase, indicating if you should move forward, backward or stay at your receiving home behind the baseline.

Once you have judged where to be, use small steps as you near the spot where you will hit the ball. Allow the ball to come to you. Aim to create space between you and the ball so that you will hit it out in front of you, hip to waist high, allowing you to execute a technically good stroke. Taking small steps allows for quick micro-adjustments right before impact, in case the ball has a slice spin on it or behaves differently than anticipated.

Carve out time to practice judging the ball. Find a practice partner to rally with. Study the bounce.

Practice is a time when you are not concerned about scoring or open court opportunities. If you don't consciously practice this skill at every opportunity, you won't be learning it as well or as quickly as you could be for use in your match play. Developing this skill, so you become good at judging where to be after the ball bounces, will help you improve both your offense and defense on the tennis court.

Gift of Tennis

Acknowledgments

Playing tennis, having the opportunity to coach and compete, has been one of the greatest gifts in my life. I am forever grateful to my loving husband, Michael, for making this possible. Without his generous support and encouragement, I never would have started this life-changing journey.

When I signed up at the YMCA for my first tennis class, I did not realize it would be the beginning of something that would teach me so much about life. This can be largely attributed to the instruction I have received from Gyata, my coach, mentor, and friend. She has tapped something from deep inside me that I never knew was there. Her belief in me has given me the confidence and skills to share this discovery with my students. Working with her has been one of the more magical aspects of my life.

My belief in "magic"—those things we cannot explain with science—was further fortified when I met Jennifer. Beyond adding a playful personality to the pages of this book, she has offered excellent insight through her artistic lens. It has been pure pleasure working together to craft this book.

My journey has been all the richer for the teaching opportunities I've had to help other adults discover the tennis player within them. Coaching the Novice League and other students I've had the privilege to work with has been tremendously rewarding. It is particularly satisfying to teach new skills and observe the growth and joy that these players exhibit when learning something new. These experiences inspired the writing of this book.

One of the other special ingredients to my tennis happiness is being a part of the tennis family at the Manlius YMCA, led by our Racquet Sports Director Paul Laurie, whose joy of the game and enthusiasm for coaching and creating opportunities permeates the tennis program. He has always believed in and supported me for which I am very grateful.

The Manlius Y has also been home to the USTA teams I've competed with. I have thoroughly enjoyed playing with these women and men, and recognize we have created a special atmosphere that makes playing tennis feel like more than a game.

I'm grateful to my children (Liberty, Christopher, and Alex), parents, sister, and brother who have been wonderful enthusiasts and companions along my tennis journey and have endured many accounts of matches and stories of coaching from me. I've had the added joy of playing with Liberty as my doubles partner this season.

I must also give special thanks to NJ Burr and Pamela Wells for sparking the idea of the book title, as they were the players who dubbed me #giftoftennis@CoachVal, and to Art Kilgour for his time and suggestions.

Finally, I'm indebted to the *Gift of Tennis* team—Jennifer, Gyata, Tina, Shelley, and Andrea—who have helped to turn these court thoughts into something tangible that can be shared with all of you.

Acknowledgments

Gift of Tennis

About the Author

Valerie Clarke, a TPA-certified tennis instructor, teaches adult beginners and novice-level players. An avid proponent of recreational tennis, she has organized local leagues, served as coach and captain for USTA women's teams, and competed in doubles tennis.

In addition to her teaching, Valerie has created and developed more than 50 doubles tennis drills for the PlayMate ball machine with Gyata Stormon. Instructions to access and use these drills will soon be released in their instruction manual, *The Playbook Drills*.

Prior to learning tennis as an adult, Valerie lived in England where she earned her doctorate in Biochemistry at the University of Oxford. Her post-doctoral research interests led her into the field of vaccine development. During a career break to raise three children with her husband, Michael, she continued her scientific interests and love of teaching through artisan bread-making, birding, gardening, and raising chickens and monarch caterpillars.

Valerie lives in Central New York with her family.

Gift of Tennis

About the Illustrator

Jennifer has loved to doodle, design, draw and paint for as long as she can remember.

With degrees in business and fine art, Jennifer started her business, froghappy!, in 2000 in Washington DC to provide decorative painting and art in kids' rooms. She ran The Gallery of CNY, a regional art gallery in Central New York, and now has a working art studio at the historic Atwell Mill in Cazenovia. Jennifer continues with a mission to provide artwork that engages a child's imagination and sparks their curiosity for fine art.

Jennifer has a very funny and handsome husband named Chip. She thinks tennis is really cool too. *

* Jennifer coached the Cazenovia High School girls and boys varsity tennis teams during the 2013 - 2018 seasons. The girls team brought home the Sectional Champion title for the first time in 20 years. Then they did it again two more times. The boys team won their first Sectional Champion title since 1986. Jennifer was one proud coach!

Gift of Tennis

Endnotes

Court Thought "Banana Split Step"
Westermann, Ian. (2019. April 2). *Top 5 Lessons from Indian Wells* (No. 310) [Audio podcast episode]. Essential Tennis

Court Thought "Every Breath You Take"
Stormon, Gyata. (2019). *On the Ball: Doubles Tennis Tactics for Recreational Players.* (pp.16-20). USA: Kindle Direct Publishing

Court Thought "From San Juan to Yukon"
Stormon, Gyata. (2019). *On the Ball: Doubles Tennis Tactics for Recreational Players.* (pp. 215-219). USA: Kindle Direct Publishing

Court Thought "Laughter Is the Best Medicine"
Westermann, Ian. (2019. June 25). *Mental and Emotional Training for Tennis.* (No. 319) [Audio podcast episode]. Essential Tennis

Court Thought "No Place Like Home"
Stormon, Gyata. (2019). *On the Ball: Doubles Tennis Tactics for Recreational Players.* (pp.22-23, 231). USA: Kindle Direct Publishing

Court Thought "On the Line"
Westermann, Ian. (2018. July 2). *How to Handle Tennis Cheaters* (No. 290) [Audio podcast episode]. Essential Tennis

Court Thought "Slowing Down Time"
Stormon, Gyata. (2019). *On the Ball: Doubles Tennis Tactics for Recreational Players.* (pp.16-20). USA: Kindle Direct Publishing

Westermann, Ian. (2019. November 8). *Doubles Coach in Your Tennis Bag* (No. 335) [Audio podcast episode]. Essential Tennis

Court Thought "Taking Sides"
Stormon, Gyata. (2019). *On the Ball: Doubles Tennis Tactics for Recreational Players.* (pp. 32-34). USA: Kindle Direct Publishing

Court Thought "Tennis Diet"
Westermann, Ian. (2018. October 17). *Maximizing Your Tennis Training Calendar* (No. 300) [Audio podcast episode]. Essential Tennis

Court Thought "Tiebreaks"
Scales, Peter. (2018). *Mental and Emotional Training for Tennis.* (pp. 111-115). Monterey, CA: Coaches Choice

Court Thought "Warm Up Before the Warm-up"
Stormon, Gyata. (2019). *On the Ball: Doubles Tennis Tactics for Recreational Players.* (p. 221). USA: Kindle Direct Publishing

Endnotes

Gift of Tennis

Bibliography

Greenwald, Jeff. (2007) *The Best Tennis of Your Life: 50 Mental Strategies for Fearless Performance.* Cincinnati, OH: Betterway Books

Mencinger, Tomaz. *"Feel Tennis: Tennis Instruction Beyond the Obvious."* [Online videos]. www.feeltennis.net/

Scales, Peter. (2018) *Mental and Emotional Training for Tennis.* Monterey, CA: Coaches Choice

Stormon, Gyata. (2019) *On the Ball: Doubles Tennis Tactics for Recreational Players.* USA: Kindle Direct Publishing

Westermann, Ian. (2018-2019) *Essential Tennis* [Audio podcast]. Retrieved from https://essentialtennis.com/

Gift of Tennis